CRE▲TIVE
HOMEOWNER®

ULTIMATE G

Architectural Ceiling Treatments

CREATIVE HOMEOWNER®

ULTIMATE GUIDE TO

Architectural Ceiling Treatments

PLAN ▪ DESIGN ▪ BUILD

Neal Barrett

CREATIVE HOMEOWNER®, Upper Saddle River, New Jersey

COPYRIGHT © 2009

CREATIVE
HOMEOWNER®

A Division of Federal Marketing Corp.
Upper Saddle River, NJ

ULTIMATE GUIDE TO ARCHITECTURAL CEILING TREATMENTS

MANAGING EDITOR	Fran Donegan
GRAPHIC DESIGNER	Kathryn Wityk
PHOTO COORDINATOR	Robyn Poplasky
JUNIOR EDITOR	Jennifer Calvert
EDITORIAL ASSISTANT	Sara Markowitz
DIGITAL IMAGING SPECIALIST	Frank Dyer
INDEXER	Schroeder Indexing Services
COVER DESIGN	Kathryn Wityk
COVER PHOTOGRAPHY	Eric Roth

CREATIVE HOMEOWNER

VICE PRESIDENT AND PUBLISHER	Timothy O. Bakke
ART DIRECTOR	David Geer
MANAGING EDITOR	Fran J. Donegan

Current Printing (last digit)
10 9 8 7 6 5 4 3 2 1

Ultimate Guide to Architectural Ceiling Treatments, First Edition
Library of Congress Control Number: 2007942990
ISBN-10: 1-58011-414-8
ISBN-13: 978-1-58011-414-1

CREATIVE HOMEOWNER®
A Division of Federal Marketing Corp.
24 Park Way
Upper Saddle River, NJ 07458
www.creativehomeowner.com

Metric Equivalents

Length

1 inch	25.4mm
1 foot	0.3048m
1 yard	0.9144m
1 mile	1.61km

Area

1 square inch	645mm^2
1 square foot	0.0929m^2
1 square yard	0.8361m^2
1 acre	4046.86m^2
1 square mile	2.59km^2

Volume

1 cubic inch	16.3870cm^3
1 cubic foot	0.03m^3
1 cubic yard	0.77m^3

Common Lumber Equivalents

Sizes: Metric cross sections are so close to their U.S. sizes, as noted below, that for most purposes they may be considered equivalents.

Dimensional lumber	1 x 2	19 x 38mm
	1 x 4	19 x 89mm
	2 x 2	38 x 38mm
	2 x 4	38 x 89mm
	2 x 6	38 x 140mm
	2 x 8	38 x 184mm
	2 x 10	38 x 235mm
	2 x 12	38 x 286mm
Sheet sizes	4 x 8 ft.	1200 x 2400mm
	4 x 10 ft.	1200 x 3000mm
Sheet thicknesses	¼ in.	6mm
	⅜ in.	9mm
	½ in.	12mm
	¾ in.	19mm
Stud/joist spacing	16 in. o.c.	400mm o.c.
	24 in. o.c.	600mm o.c.

Capacity

1 fluid ounce	29.57mL
1 pint	473.18mL
1 quart	0.95L
1 gallon	3.79L

Weight

1 ounce	28.35g
1 pound	0.45kg

Temperature

Fahrenheit = Celsius x 1.8 + 32
Celsius = Fahrenheit - 32 x ⁵⁄₉

Nail Size and Length

Penny Size	Nail Length
2d	1"
3d	1¼"
4d	1½"
5d	1¾"
6d	2"
7d	2¼"
8d	2½"
9d	2¾"
10d	3"
12d	3¼"
16d	3½"

safety

Although the methods in this book have been reviewed for safety, it is not possible to overstate the importance of using the safest methods you can. What follows are reminders—some do's and don'ts of work safety—to use along with your common sense.

▌ Always use caution, care, and good judgment when following the procedures described in this book.

▌ Always be sure that the electrical setup is safe, that no circuit is overloaded, and that all power tools and outlets are properly grounded. Do not use power tools in wet locations.

▌ Always read container labels on paints, solvents, and other products; provide ventilation; and observe all other warnings.

▌ Always read the manufacturer's instructions for using a tool, especially the warnings.

▌ Use hold-downs and push sticks whenever possible when working on a table saw. Avoid working short pieces if you can.

▌ Always remove the key from any drill chuck (portable or press) before starting the drill.

▌ Always pay deliberate attention to how a tool works so that you can avoid being injured.

▌ Always know the limitations of your tools. Do not try to force them to do what they were not designed to do.

▌ Always make sure that any adjustment is locked before proceeding. For example, always check the rip fence on a table saw or the bevel adjustment on a portable saw before starting to work.

▌ Always clamp small pieces to a bench or other work surface when using a power tool.

▌ Always wear the appropriate rubber gloves or work gloves when handling chemicals, moving or stacking lumber, working with concrete, or doing heavy construction.

▌ Always wear a disposable face mask when you create dust by sawing or sanding. Use a special filtering respirator when working with toxic substances and solvents.

▌ Always wear eye protection, especially when using power tools or striking metal on metal or concrete; a chip can fly off, for example, when chiseling concrete.

▌ Never work while wearing loose clothing, open cuffs, or jewelry; tie back long hair.

▌ Always be aware that there is seldom enough time for your body's reflexes to save you from injury from a power tool in a dangerous situation; everything happens too fast. Be alert!

▌ Always keep your hands away from the business ends of blades, cutters, and bits.

▌ Always hold a circular saw firmly, usually with both hands.

▌ Always use a drill with an auxiliary handle to control the torque when using large-size bits.

▌ Always check your local building codes when planning new construction. The codes are intended to protect public safety and should be observed to the letter.

▌ Never work with power tools when you are tired or when under the influence of alcohol or drugs.

▌ Never cut tiny pieces of wood or pipe using a power saw. When you need a small piece, saw it from a securely clamped longer piece.

▌ Never change a saw blade or a drill or router bit unless the power cord is unplugged. Do not depend on the switch being off. You might accidentally hit it.

▌ Never work in insufficient lighting.

▌ Never work with dull tools. Have them sharpened, or learn how to sharpen them yourself.

▌ Never use a power tool on a workpiece—large or small—that is not firmly supported.

▌ Never saw a workpiece that spans a large distance between horses without close support on each side of the cut; the piece can bend, closing on and jamming the blade, causing saw kickback.

▌ When sawing, never support a workpiece from underneath with your leg or other part of your body.

▌ Never carry sharp or pointed tools, such as utility knives, awls, or chisels, in your pocket. If you want to carry any of these tools, use a special-purpose tool belt that has leather pockets and holders.

contents

8 Introduction
9 Guide to Skill Level

CHAPTER ONE

10 TYPES OF CEILING TREATMENTS
12 Paint & Wallpaper
15 Medallions & Domes
16 Molding & Cornices
18 Suspended & Plank Ceilings
20 Soffits & Lighting
22 Cove Lighting & Tin Ceilings
24 Beamed Ceilings
26 Coffered & Tray Ceilings
27 Creating a Design

CHAPTER TWO

30 TOOLS
32 General Tools
40 Specialty Tools
46 Tools for Cornices, Beams, Coffers

CHAPTER THREE

58 PAINT TECHNIQUES
60 Solid-Color Ceilings
60 Borders
62 Creating Linear Borders
64 Creating Repeating-Pattern Borders
66 Creating Stencil Borders

CHAPTER FOUR

70 WALLPAPER
72 Design Options
75 Installing a Border

CHAPTER FIVE

78 DOMES
80 Installing a Medallion
82 Ceiling Domes

CHAPTER SIX

84 APPLIED MOLDINGS
86 Molding Types
86 Installing Ceiling Molding
88 Installing Polyurethane Molding
91 Constructing a Crosscutting Jig

CHAPTER SEVEN

92 SUSPENDED CEILINGS AND CEILING TILES

94 Suspended Ceilings
96 Installing a Suspended Ceiling
99 Ceiling Tiles
100 Installing Ceiling Tiles

CHAPTER EIGHT

102 CORNICES

104 Cornice Assemblies
106 Cornice Materials

108 Cornice Installation Techniques
116 Oak Cornice with Dentils
122 Pine 6-Piece Compound Cornice
126 Cornice for Indirect Cove Lighting

CHAPTER NINE

132 PLANK CEILINGS

134 Types of Plank Ceilings
136 Installing a Plank Ceiling

CHAPTER TEN

140 TIN CEILINGS

142 Types of Panels
143 Working with Sheet Metal
145 Installing a Tin Ceiling

CHAPTER ELEVEN

150 SOFFITS

152 Soffit Design
153 Preparing Recessed Fixtures
     for Installation
154 Installing a Soffit
158 Drywall Finishing

CHAPTER TWELVE

160 BEAM CEILINGS

162 Beam Designs
164 Installing Beams

CHAPTER THIRTEEN

168 COFFERED CEILINGS

170 Coffered Designs
172 Installing a Coffered Ceiling

180 Resource Guide
182 Glossary
185 Index
189 Photo Credits

decorative ceilings

I n the vast majority of modern homes, a ceiling is simply a flat surface—most often white—that receives little attention, except when it comes time to repaint the room. Sometimes a ceiling houses recessed light fixtures or serves as a surface for mounting track lights or a chandelier, but the ceiling itself is a bit player in this drama, offering support for the other characters. Things were different in the past.

DESIGN HERITAGE

Ceiling embellishments have long been a part of most architectural traditions. Classical Roman and Greek buildings included coffered ceilings. The trend toward ceiling design continued in the Renaissance. Painted and gilded moldings can be seen in many of these ceilings, and the use of frescoes and decorative painting was common. In many cases, the ceiling became the focus of a room—consider the Sistine Chapel at the Vatican as perhaps the most well-known example.

Persian architectural styles developed their own traditions of ceiling decoration. Mosaic tiles, wooden inlay, and painted surfaces feature extremely elaborate geometric patterns. Examples of these applications can be seen throughout the Middle East and in Spain.

Ceiling tiles, right, are one option for ceiling decoration. Other techniques include beam ceilings, tin ceilings, and domes, opposite.

TODAY'S DESIGNS

These historical influences in ceiling treatments found their way to the United States. Traditional forms from many cultures have sometimes been strictly applied and, at other times, used as points of departure for new architectural styles. So while your home may have come to you with plain white ceilings, you needn't leave them that way. This book will provide you with a look at many options for ceiling treatments. Whether you are a dedicated do-it-yourself enthusiast or a homeowner looking for some ideas for your next decorating project, you will find plenty of options to consider.

GUIDE TO SKILL LEVEL

Easy. Even for beginners.

Challenging. Can be done by beginners who have the patience and willingness to learn.

Difficult. Can be handled by most experienced do-it-yourselfers who have mastered basic construction skills. Consider consulting a specialist.

12 PAINT & WALLPAPER

15 MEDALLIONS & DOMES

16 MOLDING & CORNICES

18 SUSPENDED & PLANK CEILINGS

20 SOFFITS & LIGHTING

22 COVE LIGHTING & TIN CEILINGS

24 BEAMED CEILINGS

26 COFFERED & TRAY CEILINGS

27 CREATING A DESIGN

1 types of ceiling treatments

There are many ways to enhance the ceilings in your home, ranging from simple surface upgrades to extensive rebuilding projects. And while some ceiling treatments are best installed when a house is being built, most can be considered as legitimate renovations or updates to an existing home. Some of the least intrusive changes can produce dramatic results in how you experience a room. So explore the possibilities, and if you don't have much hands-on experience, start with a modest project and advance to more ambitious undertakings as your skills and confidence grow.

PAINT & WALLPAPER

Surface decoration has a great capacity for transforming the character of a room. While a plain white ceiling doesn't present much cause for excitement, a creative color scheme on the ceiling will certainly draw attention. In its simplest incarnation, this could mean simply painting the ceiling a color that complements or contrasts with the walls in the room. Or you might use one or more accent colors to create a border around the room, either adjacent to the walls or spaced some uniform distance toward the center of the room. A further elaboration of this idea might use a stencil to form the border—either one that is available commercially or one that you make yourself to reflect a personal theme.

This same concept can be executed using wallpaper instead of paint. You can apply wallpaper to the entire ceiling in a room or just create a border with a solid or patterned paper. There are even manufacturers of hand-printed wallpaper that offer elaborately figured papers designed specifically for ceiling applications. These can be assembled to form extremely intricate patterns that suggest paneling or painted scenes (Bradbury & Bradbury, www.bradbury.com). You should expect to pay a premium for these hand-crafted papers, but the results can be spectacular. And unless you have considerable experience hanging wallpaper, this kind of installation is best left to a professional.

There are also deeply textured and embossed wall covering products that can be used on ceilings. Two of the best known examples of these materials, in use since the late 1800s, are Anaglypta, made of recycled paper and cotton, and Lincrusta, made of molded linoleum. Both of these products are offered in a variety of patterns, textures, and sizes, and they must be painted after installation. Because these materials have such a long history of use, they can be an historically correct solution to a period-specific decorating dilemma. In addition, the heavy weight of these coverings makes them a great solution for covering small cracks. Of course, this only applies to surface defects and not serious structural problems.

You can also take painted treatments in a more creative direction by applying faux and textured finishes using a variety of techniques like glazing, color-washing, rag rolling, sponging, stippling, and marbleizing. And for the ultimate in painted ceilings, you can hire an artist to create a trompe l'oeil effect on the ceiling.

TOP Go beyond plain white. Use vivid colors near or on the ceiling to draw the eye upward.

BOTTOM A wallpaper ceiling border can mimic the design used on the walls.

OPPOSITE A series of painted stencil designs creates an elegant atmosphere in this room.

MEDALLIONS & DOMES

Plaster medallions have long been used in period homes to add elegance to a room. Medallions are frequently located around a chandelier or ceiling light fixture, and many designs provide a 4-inch-diameter opening for that purpose. Otherwise, medallions of different sizes and shapes are used in a variety of ways to embellish a ceiling. A row of small medallions might be placed parallel with the walls of a room; you could locate a medallion near each corner of a room; or one very large medallion can bring the focus toward the center of a large room. Medallions are available in round, oval, square, and diamond shapes, with relatively simple and extremely ornate designs. And while plaster medallions are still available (www.decoratorssupply.com), new versions in polyurethane are more readily available, offering reduced cost, easier handling, and simpler installation (www.historichouseparts.com, www.goceilingmedallion.com, www.fypon.com). You will find both unfinished and prefinished options, ranging in size from 4 inches in diameter to over 6 feet in length.

As previously mentioned, many medallions are offered with a hole to accommodate a ceiling light fixture. But if you wish to install one of these without a light, there are rosettes available that will fill the center hole. These rosettes can also be used without a medallion, placed strategically across a ceiling, either alone or in groupings.

Domes

Domes provide some of the most remarkable options available for ceilings, but as you might expect, there are some serious limitations as to where they can be used. Since a true dome extends up into the space normally used for ceiling framing, this is not generally an option when there is a living space directly above the room. But when the structural and space requirements are not a problem, a dome is unequalled in the sense of drama and space that it can create. Domes are available in many configurations and sizes. The depth can vary from a few inches to several feet, and the diameter or length can range from as small as 3 feet to almost 20 feet. You can find both round and oval shapes and different arcs, some relatively flat, others half-spherical; most are offered with smooth interior surfaces, but you can also find some with coffered patterns. Domes are manufactured in reinforced gypsum, fiberglass, and polyurethane, sometimes with wooden trim or panels.

ABOVE Ceiling medallions can be made of plaster, but most are now formed from polyurethane.

OPPOSITE Ceiling domes add drama, but they are usually a project associated with new construction.

Because the installation of a true dome is so demanding, this type of ceiling is usually included in the initial construction of a room. But if the conditions are right, it is definitely possible to modify an existing ceiling to accept a dome—keep in mind, though, that this is not a project for the casual D-I-Y enthusiast. Structural modifications of this type should be designed by an architect or engineer and carried out by a qualified contractor.

If the idea of a dome is appealing but you can't modify the ceiling framework, there are also surface-mounted models that simulate the effect of a true dome. These have a raised ring that holds the edge of the dome away from the ceiling surface, allowing sufficient space for the arc. Of course the degree of arc is severely limited in this type of design, but the effect can still be quite attractive.

To provide the maximum in drama, light valence kits are offered with many domes. These allow you to install indirect lighting to illuminate the domed surface.

MOLDING & CORNICES

In the same way that you can apply moldings to the walls of a room to create wall frames, you can apply a single molding, or combination of profiles, to a ceiling. You could install the moldings to follow the walls of the room, create a central panel to surround a chandelier, or space a series of panels across the ceiling. This type of treatment can be as simple or as complex as you desire, and is relatively easy to install—especially if you have a willing helper. Ceiling molding applications can be designed from stock home-center moldings, or you can find dedicated ceiling moldings in either plaster or urethane resin. Fancy corner pieces are also available, so you can get a professional-quality job without having to make any miter cuts (www.wishihadthat.com).

Cornices

A cornice is a molding, or grouping of different molding profiles, that creates a transition between the wall and ceiling. This concept includes extremely simple and very complex and ornate assemblies, and everything in between. Some might argue that a cornice is not technically a ceiling treatment, but in fact, a well designed cornice brings attention to the ceiling and creates a sense of direction and focus in the room.

Some molding profiles are associated with a particular style or architectural genre, and others have been used so widely that they have no specific historical or design associations. By carefully selecting the moldings used in a cornice, you can make a powerful statement about the personality you wish to create in a room. The cornice, therefore, is useful in two distinct ways; it can provide both intellectual and purely visual cues to someone entering a room. On the intellectual side, you can identify the room, if you choose, with a recognized period or style— this immediately generates associations with other known examples of that style and places the room in an established context. And in strictly visual terms, an effective cornice presents strong lines, shadows, and interesting shapes that draw the eye, regardless of the historical reference. These are traditional tools of the designer, architect, or fine artist, and they have great power to shape the way you experience a room, subtly directing your attention in a particular direction.

■ **Cornice Designs.** When it comes time to design a cornice, you have considerable resources to consult.

Home centers or lumberyards have a substantial selection of molding profiles to view. You will find that most have some brochures from molding manufacturers that offer specific cornice designs that you can assemble from their profiles. Moldings are available in softwood and hardwood species, as well as in MDF (medium-density fiberboard), and polyurethane. There are products that are meant to be painted and others that are suitable for a clear or stained finish. For those with basic woodworking experience, you can also use a router and table saw to make your own moldings; many molding profile bits are available for the router, and the process is not particularly difficult.

And if you cannot find or make the proper moldings for a cornice to suit your room, there are many specialty millwork suppliers that are able to provide just about anything you might desire. Although you should expect to pay a premium for this type of custom work, the costs will still be relatively small when compared with a major room renovation.

OPPOSITE Ornate cornices are usually made up of multiple molding profiles.

RIGHT Polyurethane crown molding simplifies installation. Note how the design is echoed in the door casing.

BELOW Simple ceiling moldings can be used with cornices to create a sophisticated ceiling design.

Suspended ceilings are a traditional ceiling treatment for basements, but the look of many newer products allow them to be used in more formal rooms as well.

SUSPENDED CEILINGS AND ACOUSTIC TILES

Many people associate suspended ceilings and tiles with commercial and office buildings. But these products have evolved in both material and design, and they present a valid option for home ceiling renovation, offering many choices of pattern and style, coupled with convenience and ease of installation. Both types of ceiling also offer superior soundproofing qualities when compared with either drywall or plaster.

Ceiling tiles can be applied directly to a plaster or drywall surface with adhesive, or you can first mount wood furring strips to the ceiling and then use staples to mount the tiles. Although at one time this type of tile contained asbestos as one of its components, this has not been the case since the mid 1970s—today they are usually composed of wood-based fiber or recycled post-consumer and post-industrial products. Most tiles are sold as 12 x 12-inch squares with interlocking tongue-and-groove edges. A variety of styles and surface embossments is available, and most tiles will accept a painted surface, al-

lowing you to create either a subtle or a dynamic look. Other tiles are offered with metallic coatings to mimic the look of a traditional tin ceiling.

Suspended ceilings are most suitable for use in rooms with unfinished ceilings—basement renovations are the most typical application in a home. To install one of these systems, you would hang metal tracks from the ceiling joists using wires to create a grid. Manufactured panels are then laid into the grid to form the ceiling surface. The panels for a suspended ceiling are most often 2 x 4 feet or 2 x 2 feet, and they are offered in many different patterns, configurations, and colors. Some are flat, and others have recessed edges that allow them to drop below the surface of the metal tracks. There are also manufacturers of tin ceilings that sell metal panels that fit into suspended ceiling grids (American Tin Ceiling Co., www.americantinceilings.com). While suspended ceilings provide a relatively quick-and-easy way to install a finished ceiling in a basement or utility room, they provide the additional benefit of allowing easy access to pipes, heating ducts, and electrical wiring that typically run through or beneath the ceiling framing.

PLANK CEILINGS

When you consider the popularity of hardwood flooring, the extension of the concept to the ceiling isn't a big leap. In fact, you can easily apply boards to a flat or sloped ceiling to create a warm and visually compelling atmosphere in a room.

There are many different wood materials suitable for this type of application. One of the most traditional choices is 4-inch-wide boards of Douglas fir with a beaded profile milled into the face of the stock. These boards have been used for porch ceilings and as wainscoting for well over 100 years, but they are equally suited for use as an interior ceiling. As with any solid-wood product, these boards can be painted or stained, or you can simply apply a clear finish to maintain the natural color of the wood.

Knotty pine boards are also quite popular for ceiling applications. Boards are available in a variety of widths, with tongue-and-groove edges that make installation quite simple. Some pine boards are sold with a beaded profile milled on one face and a plain surface on the opposite face. This gives you the opportunity to further cus-

tomize the look of your ceiling by installing the boards to expose the face you find more attractive. You will also find a variety of packaged hardwood boards that are generally sold as wall paneling material, but you could certainly use them on the ceiling, as well. All of these products can be installed by either nailing them directly to ceiling joists or first installing furring strips over a drywall or plaster ceiling and nailing the boards to them.

Some manufacturers offer planks for ceilings that feature a prefinished laminate surface (Armstrong, www.armstrong.com). These usually have a core of medium-density fiberboard (MDF) and are installed using proprietary clips that fit into the grooved edges of the plank. The ceiling planks are available in a variety of wood-grain and painted finishes, eliminating the need to finish the material after installation.

LEFT Traditional plank ceilings are made of wood, but new versions are made of medium-density fiberboard.

ABOVE Exposed roof planks add a rustic touch to this attic bedroom.

SOFFITS

A soffit is an area of lowered ceiling, usually adjacent to the walls of a room. The most widely known application of this concept is the boxed area, immediately above many kitchen cabinets, that fills the space between the cabinets and kitchen ceiling. However, this concept needn't be limited to a kitchen or to a cabinet installation. Soffits can be built in a portion of a room to create a sense of intimacy or dedicated purpose—such as for a reading nook or workspace. In addition, a soffit can be used to house recessed fixtures that can provide general lighting for a room or directed light for artwork or a particular task.

There are no specific dimensions pertaining to how a soffit is defined; it can extend down from the general ceiling surface as little as 1 inch or more than 1 foot, and it can extend out into the room by only a few inches or several feet. One of the interesting uses of soffits is to create a sense of expanding space in the center of a room. By lowering the ceiling on the perimeter of a space, you tend to experience the central area as being considerably more open—even if it is the same height as the ceilings throughout the rest of the building.

A soffit can be constructed with the traditional framing materials of two-by lumber and/or plywood. It can be faced with drywall, plaster, tile, metal, or wood, allowing you to to determine the degree of visual impact.

LIGHTING

Lighting is a powerful tool used by architects and designers to influence the way we experience a room. Everyone is familiar with the properties of brightness and color when considering light. For example, if you walk into a room that is lit by a dim incandescent bulb, your experience is considerably different from that of being in the same room lit by bright sunlight. These qualities of light can actually alter your mood when you enter a space, and they can affect how you see objects of various colors. Scientists of many disciplines have studied how light modifies our perceptions, but you needn't be a scientist to make use of light to shape the decor of your home. By carefully considering the types of lighting you use, as well as its placement and direction, you can create the desired atmosphere to suit a particular task or occasion.

As an overview, lighting can be divided into a few categories and, often, the same types of fixtures can serve more than one purpose. Ambient lighting provides an

OPPOSITE Soffits tend to make the center of the ceiling seem higher than it really is. This soffit houses recessed ceiling fixtures.

ABOVE Most rooms require many lighting sources. This kitchen has ceiling fixtures for general lighting and hanging and under-cabinet fixtures for task lighting.

overall sense of brightness, allowing you to move around safely and see from one end of the room to the other. This can be provided by ceiling fixtures, chandeliers, sconces, track lights, or floor and table lamps. Task lighting directs light for a particular purpose—like reading, writing, or working at a kitchen counter—with the intention of making those jobs easier or safer. Lamps, track lights, spots, and pendant fixtures are most often used to target these needs. And accent lighting helps to provide drama by bringing attention to decorative objects or creating an unusual visual effect. The key elements in this category are track lighting, recessed ceiling fixtures, sconces, and cove lighting.

COVE LIGHTING

Cove lighting refers to a system of indirect lighting that is housed in a cornice or soffit close to the ceiling. Because the light can only shine upward, it illuminates the top few inches of the walls and the ceiling at its perimeter, creating a sense of warmth and the illusion that the ceiling is higher than it truly is. There are many ways to approach the concept of cove lighting, and many choices in the types of light sources you can use.

Fluorescent light fixtures have been considered the standard for cove lighting, due to their energy efficiency, long life, and low operating temperatures. However, fluorescent light has long been associated with commercial and office environments, moslty because it usually is not as warm as people like for their homes. Incandescent bulbs create warmer light but are not a good choice for use in cove lighting due to their size, the excessive heat they generate, and the uneven nature of the light. In addition, the relative energy inefficiency of incandescent light makes it a less attractive as conservation becomes more critical. Viable alternative light sources are now available in xenon low-voltage fixtures and LED rope and strip lights. These tiny fixtures provide many light-color and brightness options, so you should be able to design a cove lighting system that creates the effect you desire.

The structure that houses cove lighting can be created in a number of ways. If you cover the housing with drywall and paint it to match the walls in the room, it will have minimal visual impact on the appearance of the room. You can also select a prefabricated molding that is designed to house cove lighting. These moldings are offered in polyurethane and plaster and are designed to be screwed and glued to the wall surface to conceal the light fixtures. Lastly, you can construct a cornice or soffit of wood using stock lumber and moldings. This option provides you with the most flexibility in designing your lighting system, allowing you to pick the profiles used and the finish you will apply. For a more modest impact, you can paint the assembly to match or complement the wall or ceiling colors; to create an attention-getting feature in the room, you can stain or clear-finish the moldings.

Cove lighting makes the ceiling appear higher than it actually is. This perimeter lighting is more decorative than functional and imparts a cozy feeling to the entire room.

TIN CEILINGS

Tin ceiling panels first became available during the second half of the nineteenth century and were commonly used in both residential and commercial construction until the beginning of the second World War. They first were developed as a less expensive alternative to the artistic plaster ceiling decoration that was prevalent in finer homes and public buildings. And as more and more products of the industrial revolution established a sound footing in the culture, this type of interior embellishment gained in popularity, fueled by the highly wrought architectural style that became known as Victorian.

The suburban housing boom of the 1950s, '60s, and '70s had no place for tin ceilings in the stripped-down style that was predominant. But now this type of ceiling decoration has a new life, fueled largely by renewed interest in historic housing and renovation of urban buildings. One nice feature of tin ceilings is that they can be applied quite simply over a wide range of existing surfaces. Compared with other treatments, they remain affordable, and this is a project that often does not require professional installation. Tin panels can also be applied in combination with other treatments, such as beamed and coffered ceilings, providing a rich, layered surface that can be tailored to fit your personal design scheme.

Once a common building material in middle-class homes, tin ceilings are making a comeback. Panels come prefinished or with no finish at all.

Panels for tin ceilings are created by pressing metal panels in shaped molds. Originally these panels were tin-plated steel, but now aluminum, copper, and stainless steel are also available. You will find panels that are prefinished with paint, clear lacquer, or antiqued surfaces, or you can choose panels that have no finish. (Go to www.abbingdon.com, www.classicceilings.com, www.americantinceilings.com, www.thetinman.com.) Panels come in a variety of sizes and patterns, and cornice moldings of matching or complementary patterns are also available.

For standard installation of a tin ceiling, you first attach either furring strips or a solid layer of construction plywood to the ceiling. Then you establish layout lines. The last step is to just follow the lines and nail the panels in place. Panels are designed to overlap the adjacent piece to create a seamless appearance. If you have a suspended ceiling, there are also metal panels available with recessed edges, made to fit the support tracks. You can simply place them into the ceiling grid, holding the panels flat against the track with concealed clips.

BEAMED CEILINGS

Beamed ceilings first appeared as a result of their structural function as supporting elements in post-and-beam construction. In a true beamed ceiling, the beams carry the boards that form both the ceiling and floor above; spacing and dimension of the beams are dependent on the load they must bear. While this type of construction is still used in some buildings, especially barns, it is relatively rare in residential design. More typically, homes are built using frame construction, in which nominal two-by lumber forms the core of the walls, floor, ceiling, and roof. In frame construction, intermediary support for the ceiling members is most often provided by interior walls, with only occasional use of visible beams—and these are usually sheathed in drywall or plaster to reduce their visual impact.

Decorative beams are meant to suggest their supportive cousins, but because they have no real structural function, their design can be entirely dependent on visual factors. For large rooms with high ceilings, beams can be larger and more closely spaced; smaller spaces with low ceilings usually work better with smaller, widely spaced

beams. Beams that run across a long room tend to make the space feel wider, while those that follow the long dimension accentuate the room length. Beams can run directly between wall surfaces, or they can end at half-beams that abut the walls, suggesting supporting members at the perimeter. Likewise, you can construct one or more larger beams toward the center of the room that appear to support the cross-beams mid-span. For a simpler approach, you can limit the treatment to installing half-beams around the outside of the room, much like a cornice. You are not limited to using beams on only flat ceilings, and they can be particularly effective in rooms that feature sloped, cathedral ceilings. Beams can be oriented parallel with the rafters, following the slope of the ceiling, or parallel with the ridge board, to suggest structural purlins.

Structural beams are either solid timbers or laminated assemblies that must meet strict load-bearing requirements. In most cases, decorative beams are assembled from smaller pieces of softwood or hardwood lumber and trimmed with some kind of ceiling molding. They are constructed in a hollow, U-shaped form and hung on the ceiling from blocking strips. You then have the option of painting, staining, or clear-finishing the wood surfaces. This type of decorative beam would tend to be a prominent feature in a room. Alternately, you could face beams with drywall or plaster and then apply paint or wallpaper to them. This treatment would emphasize the structure over the beam surface and would likely be a more subtle presence in the overall room design.

For those who aren't interested in the mess or expense of installing real wood or drywall beams, there is another alternative: decorative beams of polyurethane, which feature surfaces that suggest rustic solid-wood beams but at a fraction of the cost and weight (www.fauxwood-beams.com). Most of these beams are prefinished, allowing you to bypass the finishing steps, as well. As with decorative wood beams, these plastic "beams" are hung from blocks fastened to the ceiling surface.

OPPOSITE TOP Beams appear to lengthen the room in the direction they run.

OPPOSITE BOTTOM Log homes rely on decorative or structural beams to provide authenticity to the design.

RIGHT These stained beams complement the vivid color of the kitchen cabinetry.

BELOW Use beams in combination with other decorative ceiling techniques. Here, the bright white beams set off the color of the main ceiling area.

COFFERED CEILINGS

A coffered ceiling is constructed in much the same way as a beamed ceiling. However, instead of the beams running only in one direction, they are arranged so that they intersect, forming recessed areas enclosed by beams. The recessed areas are called coffers. In practice, these can take many different forms. Coffered ceilings can be formed entirely of plaster or drywall, or they can consist of wooden beams with a plaster or drywall ceiling. The intersecting beams can be of uniform depth, or those running in one direction can be deeper and/or wider, suggesting support for the thinner members. Beams can be simple or ornate, with single or layered moldings applied against the ceiling. And the ceiling of a coffer can be painted, wallpapered, or surfaced with wooden boards, veneer, or tin ceiling panels.

These designs most often feature square or rectangular coffers. However, it is also possible to create diamond-shaped coffers by running beams diagonally across a room. And for even more elaborate treatments, circular, oval, or polygonal coffers can be located in the center of a room with radiating beams extending toward the walls. Whatever the configuration, coffered ceilings are usually reserved for the more formal, public rooms of a home—a library or a dining or living room, for example.

TRAY CEILINGS

Tray ceilings are so named because they tend to resemble an inverted tray, with sides that either slope or step up from the perimeter walls in the room toward the main flat ceiling surface. These ceilings are quite tall, due to the height requirements of the transitional surfaces, so they are rarely used when there is a living space directly above the room. It is most common for tray ceilings to be built as an element in new construction, but it is possible to add this feature as part of a renovation in a ranch-style home or a second-floor room directly below the attic.

A tray ceiling design presents a number of opportunities for embellishment. The sloped or stepped portion of the ceiling is a natural space for contrasting paint or wallpaper treatments. And the additional intersecting planes present perfect locations for decorative moldings. Recessed lighting can also be added, either as cove lighting or as a built-in feature of the design.

Due to the complex structural features of a tray ceiling, this type of project is usually beyond the capability of even a dedicated D-I-Y homeowner.

TOP LEFT Coffered ceilings add a formal appearance to any room design.

BELOW Tray ceilings offer the opportunity for a variety of surface-finishing techniques.

CREATING A DESIGN

Home ownership provides the freedom to create whatever type of living environment one would like, but most often homeowners choose to maintain a sense of consistent design. Some buildings, especially those built before the middle of the twentieth century, belong to a clearly defined architectural genre. For instance, Georgian, Federal, or Victorian houses are easy to identify, and it's common to keep the interior design consistent with period details appropriate to the form. However, if your home is of a more modern tradition or part of a mid- to late-twentieth-century suburban housing development—and lacking in compelling architectural details—you have, most likely, created a unique atmosphere with your own decorative touches and furnishings. These details and motifs are the first things to consider when searching for direction in ceiling embellishment. Try to design a treatment that is consistent with the spirit of the prevailing style, even if it doesn't strictly adhere to the formal rules of a specific design or architectural school of thought.

If your home features a particular molding profile as window or door casing, for example, you might consider using a similar profile as part of a cornice. Or for a house that is built in the Victorian style, you could add a coffered ceiling with elaborate, layered moldings and period-wallpapered panels. In a residence that reflects the Arts and Crafts aesthetic, a simple beamed ceiling using the same wood species as the interior trim might be appropriate. Of course, there are no strict rules for these decisions, but in general, you are on safe ground if the ceiling seems in harmony with the overall environment of the home.

Even if you are not concerned with adhering to a particular architectural discipline, it's good to evaluate the suitability of a project when you think about a renovation, if only in the most general sense of period style versus contemporary design. Some treatments are more appropriate for buildings of a certain period and seem out of place in another context. Domed ceilings, medallions, or applied surface moldings, for instance, are characteristic of older or more traditional architecture, while skylights and track-lighting fixtures are often found in modern residences. Although these issues may not weigh heavily in your own decorative decisions, it is wise to think about how your project might affect the value of your home and its appeal to potential buyers.

Some house designs, such as this post-and-beam home, already contain ceiling embellishments.

Structural versus Surface Modifications

In the broadest sense, ceiling treatments can be divided into two categories. The first group includes items that are purely decorative and involve only surface application, such as applied moldings or paint and wallpaper treatments. Some embellishments in this category, like a coffered or tin ceiling, might require considerable fabrication and installation work, but they don't actually change the framework of the building.

The second group includes modifications that either have a structural component, such as weight-bearing beams, or require modifications to the framing members in the room, such as a domed ceiling. If you plan to undertake an improvement that affects the structure of the building, it is always a good idea to consult with an engineer or architect in the earliest stages of the project—this is especially important when planning changes to a room that has living space above it. Keep in mind that the framework for a ceiling can also be the support for the floor above, and even small changes could compromise the structure. An engineer or architect can give you a true idea of the work and costs involved in your job. They often have access to materials and strategies that can address problems that seem impossible to resolve. Of course, there are also times when they might need to let you know that an intended improvement is ill-advised; in these cases they will likely present an alternative plan that you may not have otherwise considered. When undertaking one of these projects, it's often best to consign the structural changes to a professional contractor, leaving the more decorative elements for you to complete yourself at a later date.

Room Size and Ceiling Height

The type and details of your ceiling modifications are affected by many factors, but two primary considerations are the size of the room and the height of the ceiling. In general, there is a direct relationship between these dimensions—larger rooms demand higher ceilings and smaller rooms function better with lower ceilings. In most cases, a large public room, such as a living room, will feel cramped and claustrophobic if the ceiling is too low, and a small room, such as a bathroom, with a high ceiling will have poor acoustics and can seem like a dungeon.

Despite this general rule, there are times when different ceiling heights can be used effectively within a single room. Dropped ceilings or alcoves can provide an interesting use of space, defining an area for a particular use. This is especially effective along the edges of a large living room or great room. For instance, a corner that is dedicated to reading or watching television can be made more intimate by lowering the ceiling. Conversely, a sense of expanded space in the center of a room can be created by adding a soffit around the perimeter; this technique is particularly useful in a kitchen or bathroom.

EVALUATING EXISTING CONDITIONS

■ **Acoustic Tile.** If your project involves a room that has suspended or applied acoustic ceiling tiles instead of plaster or drywall, you will need to remove the tiles before moving on to a new installation. To remove a suspended ceiling, lift the tiles out of the grid, cut and remove the wire hangers and suspended grid, and remove the perimeter channel from the walls. Most applied tiles come in either 12 x 12-inch or 12 x 24-inch panels, with tongue-and-groove interlocking edges. They are usually

TOP Many ceiling treatments, such as medallions, require that you locate the existing ceiling joists.

BOTTOM To deconstruct a suspended ceiling, remove the tiles from the grid, and then cut away the grid.

installed by stapling them to wood furring strips that are spaced 12 inches on center. Because the tiles are quite soft, it's a simple matter to cut through them with a utility knife and pull them away from the furring. Occasionally, tiles are glued directly to the underlying ceiling. In this case removal will require more work, but if you use a flat pry bar, the tiles should come free easily. Some tiles manufactured before the mid-1970s contain asbestos. So before you begin any removal, contact your regional EPA office, state environmental office, or local health department for advice on testing, proper handling, and disposal of the material.

■ **Joists and trusses.** For any project that requires fastening material to the ceiling—such as molding, medallions, beams, or wood and tin panels—you will need to locate the framing members under the surface. In traditional frame construction, ceiling and floor joists are nominal two-by lumber, spaced 16 inches on center. If your room has no usable living space directly above it, it is likely that the ceiling joists will be 2x6 lumber. However, if the ceiling joists must also function as floor joists for a room above, you can expect that the material will be 2x8, 2x10, or even 2x12 stock.

In some instances, you may find that a ceiling is supported by trusses. These are structural framing members that are engineered so that they can span large distances while being supported only at their ends. They can be used as combination roof-ceiling framing, replacing traditional rafters and ceiling joists, or as dedicated floor trusses. In both cases they allow architects to design open floor plans with much less consideration of where to place interior load-bearing walls. In contrast to traditional framing members, trusses are usually spaced 24 inches on center.

When deciding on a ceiling treatment, consider the height of the existing ceiling. These beams increase the sense of intimacy around the informal eating area.

32 GENERAL TOOLS

40 SPECIALTY TOOLS

46 TOOLS FOR CORNICES,
BEAMS, COFFERS

2 tools

If you are interested in tackling a ceiling improvement project, you will definitely need some tools for the job. Because the nature of these improvements can vary from simple paint and paper to serious remodeling, there are quite a few tools that might be appropriate. While it would be impossible to give a comprehensive discussion of all possible implements you could use, a brief overview of the most likely candidates should be helpful. As you consider possible ceiling treatments, you will see that some tools are common to many of these projects, and these are the tools that you would likely consider as your first purchases. Once you have assembled, and mastered, these basic tools, you can then approach those items you will need for a more specific ceiling treatment.

GENERAL TOOLS

Measuring Tape

A retractable steel tape is the primary tool you will use for measuring rooms or just about any distance of more than a few feet. Tapes come in a variety of lengths and widths, but for general, all-around use a 1-inch-wide blade and 25-foot length is best. The most common design includes markings every $1/16$ inch for the entire length of the tape, with particular emphasis on every "foot" measurement and also a contrasting color or arrow to note every increment of 16 inches— the standard spacing of studs and ceiling joists. Look for a tape that also features a locking lever to keep the blade extended and also a belt clip so that you can keep the tool handy.

Folding Stick Rule

For those jobs where a flexible measuring tape is too awkward, a folding stick rule can be the perfect substitute. These rules are made of a series of $1/8$-inch-thick x 8-inch-long slats that are hinged together, folding into a compact package. You will find folding rules that are offered in lengths of either 6 or 8 feet. Most models include a sliding metal extension at one end so that you can take accurate inside measurements—this is particularly hard to do with a measuring tape.

Squares

The concept of "square" is extremely important in carpentry; two surfaces are square if they are perfectly perpendicular to one another—with the angle between them exactly 90 degrees. The tool that is used to test this quality is also called a square. Squares come in a variety of styles, sizes, and materials, depending on the particular use they are designed to fulfill. For general household use, however, the framing square is probably the most valuable. A framing square is made of either steel or aluminum and has two arms: one 16 inches long, called the tongue; and one 24 inches long, called the blade. Designed to be used in house framing, the square has a table for calculating the length of roof rafters, but its use extends far beyond that particular task. You will find it handy for checking if inside and outside corners are square, and also as a straightedge, for testing surfaces and layout.

If you are planning a cornice or other trim job, you might consider purchasing a sliding combination square as well. This tool has a $4\frac{1}{2}$-inch-long body that slides along a 12-inch blade. The body can lock in place at any point along the blade, allowing you to use it as a depth or marking gauge as well as a square. The body also has a milled edge that sits at an angle of 45 degrees to the blade; this is useful for checking miter cuts.

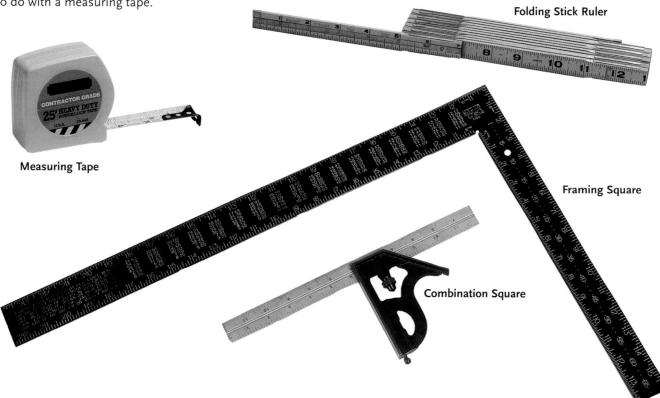

Folding Stick Ruler

Measuring Tape

Framing Square

Combination Square

Levels

In many disciplines related to building, the notions of level and plumb are foundational principles—they are relied upon to give direction and orientation to that which follows. Something is considered to be level if it is perfectly horizontal, with no slope, left or right, forward or backward. If an object is perfectly vertical, it is said to be plumb. The primary tool used to test these qualities is the spirit level. Levels come in many sizes, from a 9-inch torpedo level to a 6-foot level specifically designed for hanging doors. The most useful size, however, is the 4-foot level. Now, in many ceiling projects, you will not need to check if the ceiling is level, as it has little bearing on decorative applications, but some items could require this test. For instance, if a ceiling in an old house slopes more than 1 inch across its length, you might need to make adjustments in a cornice to avoid the feeling that you are in a "fun house" when you enter the room.

A 4-foot level can also be an extremely valuable tool when used as a straightedge, to test a wall or ceiling for bumps and hollow areas. You can use it to guide a pencil when laying out a long straight line, or to guide a utility knife for cutting wallpaper or ceiling tiles.

Chalk Line

Careful layout of a job is critical to the ultimate execution of the project, for without accurate guides, your installation will inevitably be sloppy. And in many different types of ceiling projects, marking straight lines is the primary layout task. Whether your job is to apply wallpaper, install a suspended or tin ceiling, or build a cornice, you will need to first establish some straight lines—and a chalk line is one of the quickest ways to mark a straight line between two distant points.

The tool consists of a small metal or plastic container with a reel that holds a cotton string; the string has a hook on its free end. Pour powdered chalk into the container, and then stretch the string between two points—you can hook the free end on a nail driven into one of the points. Holding the string taut, gently lift and release the line, allowing it to snap against the surface, creating a mark.

One caution: the chalk line is not the best choice for marking straight lines for painted borders because the chalk can be difficult to cover with paint and can necessitate extra coats.

Level

Chalk-Line Box

Marking Chalk

Graph Paper

For any category of ceiling improvement, it is always critical that you plan the job carefully and thoroughly. If you cannot visualize exactly where you are headed, it is highly doubtful that you will be happy with the end results of your considerable efforts. So always make it a policy to begin the job with a well-thought-out plan. One of the simplest tools to use in the early stages of a job is a pad of graph paper: it allows you to quickly draw a scaled representation of the ceiling on which you can plot your project. This applies whether the job is a stenciled or wallpaper border, tin or tile installation, or putting up a series of medallions. A scaled drawing will give you an accurate picture of how the proposed changes will actually look; it will also give you the opportunity to test various layouts and even entirely different types of ceiling treatments without going through a lot of extra work.

Stud Finder

Even though most ceiling treatments are more decorative than structural in nature, many projects do require you to fasten some elements to the wall or ceiling framing members with either nails or screws. And because the studs or ceiling joists are hidden behind a plaster or drywall sur-

face, you need some way to locate them. Of course, you can drill a series of small holes in an area until you hit something solid, but a simpler and less messy solution is to use an electronic stud finder. These tools have a sensor to detect a difference in capacitance to find the studs or ceiling joists. Most models feature a combination of lights and sounds to alert you when the tool is over a framing member.

Hammer and Nail Sets

We all know a hammer as the primary tool of the carpenter, used for driving and pulling nails. And while it often appears to be a brute instrument, in the hands of an experienced user it can also be a tool of considerable subtlety, used to coax a stubborn part into position or to gently close the seam in a tin ceiling. There are many styles and sizes of hammers from which to choose. But for all-around use by a homeowner, a 16-ounce claw hammer, with either a straight or curved claw, is the best option. You will find hammers with shafts of steel, wood, or fiberglass, and each has its advocates, but it is also generally acknowledged that no one system is best for all users. As with most tool selections, you will find that individual preference is the most compelling factor; if you have the opportunity, test each available option and choose the one that feels most comfortable.

A nail set is a hardened steel rod that is used to drive a

Electronic Stud Finder

Nail Sets

For professional-quality results, drive nailheads below the surface of the wood using a hammer and nail set.

finishing nail below the wood surface. One end of the tool is tapered to a particular diameter that fits into a recess in the nailhead. Sets are made in a variety of sizes to fit different gauge nails, so always use the proper size for the nails you are using. A set that is the wrong size can slip off of the nailhead and damage the adjacent surface.

Utility Knife

As you get involved in repairs or upgrades to your home, you will find that one of the simplest tools is also one of the most useful and versatile, and that is a small knife. As you browse the tool department of your home center or hardware store, you will find that there are many styles of knives available. But for general use, a basic re-tractable utility knife is hard to beat. A utility knife consists of a compact metal case with a slide mechanism that holds the knife blade. The slide can lock in a closed or open position so that you can be secure in knowing where the blade is—an important safety consideration. The blades are standard size, reversible, disposable, and inexpensive, so you can always have a razor-sharp edge when you need one. And most models have a storage space inside the handle for several spare blades.

You will be surprised at how frequently you will reach for the utility knife when working on a home-improvement project. The knife is handy for a wide range of jobs, from pencil sharpening and trimming wallpaper to carving a molding joint or cutting drywall.

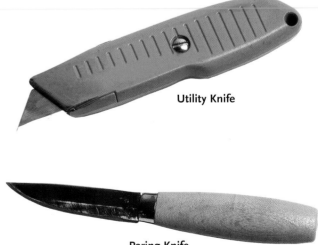

Utility Knife

Paring Knife

Drywall Saw

When it comes to cutting building materials, there seems to be a saw that is designed for just about every job. So depending on your project, you might consider one of the more particular tools as a likely purchase. But if you are planning one of the many types of ceiling improvement, there is a pretty good chance that you will get involved in some drywall repair or installation. In addition to a basic utility knife, a drywall saw is an important tool to have.

A drywall saw is a hand tool that consists of a relatively short blade with a pointed end and rather large, and widely set, teeth. You will find models with a straight handle and others with a pistol-grip handle—either type will perform perfectly well. The pointed end allows you to simply push the blade into the drywall to start a cut; there is no drilling or preparation necessary. This is particularly useful when making a cutout for an electrical box or repair in the center of a ceiling.

Pry Bars and Putty Knives

Whether your job is of a constructive or destructive nature, a pry bar can be your best friend. For general use, consider a small selection of flat bars in various sizes ranging from 4 inches to 12 inches in length. The thin blade of a bar is often the perfect tool to slip into a narrow opening without damaging the adjacent wall surface and coax an old molding to come loose. Or you can use it to persuade a piece of drywall into position when no other tool will do the job. And when even a pry bar is too thick to fit into a tiny crack, you might consider having a small putty knife to supplement the collection. Of course, you would probably not use the same knife for its named purpose, because it might suffer some bends or nicks in its use as a gentle—or not so gentle—lever.

Putty Knife   **Drywall Saw**   **Pry Bars**

Handsaw and Circular Saw

In the course of making some ceiling improvements, you may be called upon to cut some wood, perhaps to build a small scaffolding or bench, or to trim a piece of plywood or molding. And when this sort of task arises, you should be prepared with a tool that will do the job accurately and efficiently. For a small investment, you can purchase an all-purpose handsaw such as the one in the photo. This saw is equipped with aggressive teeth for cutting either with or across the grain of the wood. A handsaw is a good choice if your cutting jobs are limited in scope, because using one requires you to expend considerable energy if a lot of cutting is required.

For jobs that involve a large amount of cutting, a portable circular saw is usually the tool of choice. Saws are rated by the power of the motor and diameter of the blade. The majority of household jobs can be handled by a saw with a rating of 12-15 amps and a 7$\frac{1}{4}$-inch-diameter blade. You can expect the saw to be adjustable for depth and angle of cut, and most models will cut stock up to 2$\frac{1}{2}$ inches thick when set at 90 degrees. If the saw you choose does not come equipped with an accessory rip guide, you should consider purchasing one, especially if you know you will need to make a series of relatively narrow, long cuts. The guide will provide a measure of accuracy and safety that is extremely important with this type of tool. Specially engineered blades are available for particular jobs—ripping, crosscutting, or trimming plywood, for example—each with a different number of teeth and also with a distinctive tooth design. But to start, you can purchase a combination blade that should provide satisfactory results in most situations.

Circular Saw

Handsaw

Cordless Drill/Driver and Assorted Drill Bits

If you purchase a combination cordless drill/screwdriver, it is almost guaranteed to become one of your favorite tools. As the primary member of the ever-growing cordless tool family, it has set the standard for utility and convenience. There are two basic designs offered—inline and pistol grip. For light duty use, the inline models are fine, but for serious jobs, the pistol grip design is the tool of choice.

You can expect these tools to offer a fixed clutch setting for drilling and a number of adjustable clutch settings for screws. The adjustable clutch feature will allow you to drive screws so that the heads are set perfectly flush with the surrounding material surface, without having to worry about stripping out the pilot hole or breaking off the screw head. Keyless chucks are standard, providing you with the ability to change bits quickly without having to keep track of an easily misplaced chuck key. Extra-powerful models are available for professional use, but for most homeowners a 12 or 14.4 volt rating is sufficient. While most drills will come with a battery charger as part of the kit, you might consider the purchase of a spare battery so that you can still use the tool while the primary battery recharges.

Some drill bits are designed specifically for a certain job or for only drilling a particular material, and there are times when you may need to purchase one of those dedicated bits. But for many jobs, when drilling in wood or soft metals, like aluminum, copper, brass, or cast iron, a set of high-speed steel twist bits will be just what you want. A typical set will offer an assortment of sizes in a metal or plastic case that makes it easy to identify the size and also to keep track of the bits.

Caulk Gun

In many projects, you will be dealing with joints between dissimilar materials. This is particularly true when installing wood or urethane moldings or tin ceiling panels. And no matter how careful your installation, it is inevitable that some gaps will remain between the walls or ceiling and the new decorative elements—hollows or bumps in the drywall or plaster surface or some inflexibility in the applied material ensure that this is an expected event and part of the installation process. Even when joints seem tight initially, the different rates of expansion and contraction of the materials will cause gaps to open eventually. Fortunately, the solution comes in an inexpensive and convenient package, the caulk tube. Caulk is latex- or silicone-based crack filler that comes in a cardboard tube with a long, thin plastic nose. To apply the filler to a gap, you place the tube into a specially designed application gun. You then cut the nose to create an appropriately sized hole and, holding the nose against the gap, squeeze the trigger to push the caulk out.

While caulk has the ability to coax a less than perfect job into acceptability, it should not be thought of as a cure-all for sloppy work. Large gaps and ill-fitting joints may seem to disappear with a healthy glob of caulk, but in time, these problems will become visible. As a general rule, gaps larger than $1/8$ inch between walls and moldings and those larger than $1/16$ inch in similar-material joints should be made to fit properly before you consider the caulk solution.

You will find a number of different designs for caulk guns, some that cost as little as $2, made of thin sheet steel, and others that run as high as $12 or $15. For a small job or one-time use, one of the cheaper guns will be fine. But if you plan on holding onto the gun for many years of use, it pays to invest in the more-substantial tool—you will find it easier to control the size of the bead of caulk, and the gun will be less likely to jam in mid-use. For a painted finish, it is recommended that you apply a coat of primer to all surfaces before applying the caulk. Then let the caulk cure, following the manufacturer's instructions, before applying paint. For those jobs that will not be painted, colored and clear caulks are available and can be left just as they come from the tube.

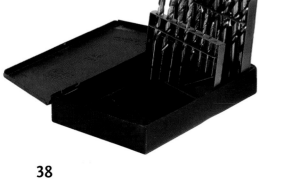

Drill Bit Set

Drill/Driver

Drop Cloths

Many home-improvement projects are messy, but ceiling projects are especially so. It's just hard to contain the dust and debris from a project when you are working overhead. For most ceiling jobs, you will need to remove at least some of the furniture from the room before you start. But there may be some pieces that are too hard to move, or you just may not have an alternative place to put them. Even when the furniture is gone, you will need to shield the floors or carpeting from damage. This is the time to invest in some good-quality drop cloths to cover those surfaces that need protection. You will find drop cloths made of either plastic or canvas, and if your budget can stand it, the canvas option is best. These are not as slippery as the plastic variety, and they are much less likely to rip. A good-quality canvas drop cloth will stand up to many years of tough use and can be vacuumed or washed, if necessary.

Ladders and Scaffolding

The prime factor that distinguishes ceiling work from any other home improvement is that you are constantly working overhead. This element of the job should be taken quite seriously because it determines much about the logistics of the task and the degree of physical exertion and flexibility that it will require. This is not to imply that you need to be an Olympic athlete to paint your ceiling, but there is no denying that ceiling work is physically demanding.

With this in mind, it is worthwhile to provide a convenient and safe way to reach the ceiling, and this usually means a stepladder. You will find stepladders in a variety of heights, materials, and designs. For work on a typical 8- or 9-foot-high ceiling, a 6-foot stepladder is ideal. Generally, aluminum ladders are the lightest, followed by fiberglass and then wood, and more weight generally corresponds to an increase in stability. Typical 6- or 8-foot stepladders have a small fold-down shelf near the top step that is handy for holding a can of paint or other tools. This can be a very useful option, eliminating the need for extra trips up and down the ladder. Certain ladders are designed with a platform and handrail at the top; this can be helpful for some jobs but can limit its flexibility for other tasks.

One interesting variation in ladder design is the articulating ladder. These models have locking joints along their length so that they can be used as either straight ladders or step ladders. You can adjust them to have front and back legs of different length so that working in a stairway is much simpler. And some models can function as a combination ladder and scaffold support, providing you with an extended work platform. Note: for use as a scaffold, you will need to either purchase the proprietary scaffolding boards or use heavy lumber planks to provide the walkway.

For large, involved ceiling projects, you might need to consider either building or renting a scaffold system. You will find rolling scaffold units, usually in 6-foot-long x 3-foot-wide sections with locking wheels at most rental centers. These can make a tough job much more approachable, by eliminating the need to constantly climb up and down a ladder and by providing a wide, stable platform from which to work.

Articulating Ladder

SPECIALTY TOOLS

It's often hard to categorize tools by specific jobs because there is naturally some overlap in the utility of any given implement. In some cases, it's obvious that a tool has many different applications, and at other times, some potential uses may be more obscure. However, there are some tools that are clearly designed for a particular task, and inversely, there are some jobs that require specialty tools. So if you are planning a ceiling project, you should definitely anticipate these needs. Here are some of the more particular, job-specific items.

Painting Tools

As home improvements go, painting is one of the most approachable types of projects you can consider. For the most part, the tools and techniques are pretty direct and decidedly low-tech, requiring little in the way of exotic implements. However, for the job to go smoothly, and to ensure the best results, it pays to invest in good-quality brushes, rollers, and roller covers.

As a result of environmental regulations, most alkyd, or oil-based, paints are being phased out for residential use; this leaves acrylic and latex paints as the coatings of choice for walls, ceiling, and trim. **Brushes** that are recommended for these water-based paints have synthetic bristles, usually nylon or polyester or a blend of the two. When shopping for brushes, look for those with long, tapered bristles, longer in the center than toward the edge of the brush. This shape encourages the paint to spread smoothly and evenly. The bristles should also have split, also called flagged, ends—these feathered tips are more flexible and will create a smooth finish. Finally, the bristles should be longer than the brush is wide because the extra length also provides more flexibility. This allows the paint to flow easily onto the surface and encourages an easier and less aggressive stroke. As a general rule, the bristles should be 1½ times as long as the width of the brush. A selection of two or three different-sized brushes will serve you well for most jobs. Consider a 3-inch-wide brush for general wall or ceiling applications, including cutting in at corners and trim, and a 1 or 1½-inch-wide angled bristle brush for trim and detail work.

Rollers are often the preferred tool for applying paint to large, flat surfaces—especially ceilings. Look for a solid, good-quality roller frame that accepts an extension handle so that you can stand on the floor and still reach the ceiling. As with brushes, **roller covers** for latex paint are synthetic material and will be clearly marked for the appropriate type of paint. For smooth surfaces like drywall or plaster, you can purchase covers with a short nap, ¼ or ½ inch, but for uneven surfaces like rough paneling or a textured ceiling, a longer nap cover, ¾ or even 1-inch, will provide the best coverage. You will also need a roller tray to hold the paint; you will find metal and plastic models available—if you buy a good-quality tray, it can last a lifetime. Although you will also find disposable trays or tray liners, it usually takes only a few minutes to wash out a tray at the end of a job, so it's hard to justify the extra waste generated by the disposable products.

Paint Tray and Rollers

Brushes

Paint Spray Gun

Although brush and roller applications are most common for interior paint, you can also consider a spray gun for large areas. Professional painters frequently use spray guns to quickly get paint onto a surface—often followed by brushing or rolling to ensure smooth and even coverage. For the homeowner, small airless units are available at relatively reasonable cost. These light-duty sprayers often require you to thin the paint before spraying. Or you can check with your local rental center as they often have heavy-duty units that will spray latex coatings without thinning.

A successful paint job depends as much on proper preparation as on the actual application of the paint. Masking surfaces that will not be painted is one of these steps, and it's worth paying particular attention to this part of the job, as it can save you considerable effort in cleanup and eliminate the need for extensive touch-ups as well. If you are planning a ceiling border, masking is the primary technique for defining the limits of the design, so careful layout and application of the mask is essential. **Masking tape** is the principal tool for protecting these adjacent surfaces, and you will find it offered in a number of different grades and sizes. For most paint jobs you should look for low-tack tape, often colored blue or green. This tape will adhere to other painted surfaces but will not cause damage when pulled away. If you use a wide strip of masking tape, you can also use the outer edge of the tape to fasten a wide paper mask or plastic drape to further protect an adjacent area from splatters or drips.

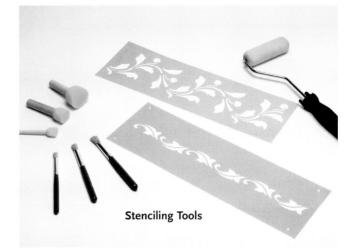

Stenciling Tools

For jobs that include a **stenciled border** on your ceiling, you have a few options. First, you can look for stencils at a local craft supply or specialty paint store. These businesses often carry an assortment of stencils and stencil tools, some that are especially designed for walls or ceilings, and others for general arts and crafts purposes that can be adapted to ceiling use. For a more extensive selection, there are specialty suppliers that you can find online or in catalogs (www.stencilsearch.com, www.victorialarsen.com).

Of course, you always have the option of fabricating your own stencil designs. You can consult pattern books for inspiration or use a personal theme or image as the basis of your design. Stencils can be made of smooth cardboard or soft linoleum, vinyl, or Mylar sheets, available from craft or art suppliers. Simply draw the desired design onto the stencil material; then use a razor-sharp utility knife to cut out the pattern. Remember to place the stencil on a disposable cardboard backer so that you do not ruin the table underneath.

While you could use a general-purpose paintbrush to apply paint to a stencil, you will get better results, and the job will be easier, if you purchase a set of short-bristle stencil brushes. This type of brush will give you much more control of the application process, because you won't need to worry about long bristles straying outside the parameters of the stencil, and there will be much less chance of excess paint drips. In addition to bristle brushes, you will also find sponge brushes that are specifically designed for stencil use. Either of these tools is especially useful when your stencil includes a multicolor or variegated design. For solid-color stencils, you can also use a small roller to apply the paint.

Blue Painter's Tape

Wallpapering Tools

Wallpaper offers a vast range of design possibilities for ceiling decoration. At the simple end of the spectrum is the application of a uniform pattern across the entire ceiling. More-complex ideas might include the use of a **wallpaper border** on a painted ceiling, a solid wallpapered field with a contrasting border, or even an assembly of several different papers to form an intricate geometric or pictographic design. You will find suppliers of wallpaper borders either online or through dedicated paint and wallpaper dealers. Borders offer you the ability to personalize your room decor by bringing a meaningful theme or visual image into the ceiling design.

Wallpapering Tools

When undertaking a wallpaper job, there are a handful of special tools that you will need. You should be able to find these tools at a home center or hardware store or from a paint and wallpaper specialty store. If you do not have access to any of these, there are mail-order suppliers who will ship these tools anywhere (www.paintstoreonline.com, www.advance-equipment.com).

First, you will need a place to work—a flat surface that can hold the paper while you cut it and apply the paste. Although you can buy dedicated wallpaper tables, you can also just rest a piece of smooth plywood on a set of tall sawhorses instead.

Next, you will need a **knife** to cut and trim the paper. Of course, you can use a normal utility knife for this task, but for wallpaper, it is important to always have a razor-sharp edge as even a slightly dull blade could cause a tear. Rather than changing blades every few minutes, you could buy a knife with break-off blades. These blades are scored at regular intervals down their length so that you can snap off a dull section and continue to use the blade with no time lost.

Some wallpaper comes with a prepasted surface, which you must soak in a tray before installation, but most papers require you to apply paste. You can use a special **paste brush**, normal paintbrush, or foam roller for the application. Once applied to the ceiling, you will need a wide **smoothing brush** to work the paper flat onto the surface. These are typically 12 inches wide with medium-stiff bristles. As an alternative, you can also use a soft plastic **smoothing blade** for the same purpose.

For a professional-quality wallpaper job, you need to roll the seams to ensure a good bond to the ceiling surface. The proper tool for this task is a small 1- or 2-inch-wide **roller** with a short handle. You will find rollers of wood, steel, hard rubber, and plastic—any of these will do the job.

Typically wallpaper seams are made by overlapping adjacent runs of paper and, using a **straightedge** as a guide, cutting through both layers to form the joint. A selection of straightedge guides is always helpful, but you do not need to purchase a dedicated tool for this purpose; a yardstick and one or two shorter metal rulers will be sufficient for most situations.

Tools for Suspended Ceilings, Acoustic Tiles, and Tin Ceilings

Installing a suspended or tin ceiling or applying ceiling tiles are relatively low-tech projects and, as such, require little in the way of specialized tools. However, there are a few necessary items, as well as some optional ones, that you should at least consider before starting one of these jobs. Because the tracks for a suspended ceiling are made of metal, you will need a way to cut them to size—this also applies to tin ceiling panels. The best tool for this is a metal shear or **tin snips**. Because these parts are not particularly heavy gauge material, look for cutters that are easy to handle rather than an awkward shear that requires two hands to operate. When cutting tin ceiling panels, you will inevitably be left with an edge that is quite sharp. To protect your hands against nasty cuts, it is best to always wear **leather gloves**. And for those times when you need to remove a burr or slightly ease the edge of a panel or molding, an 8-inch-long **mill file** will be the perfect tool for the job.

The tracks for a suspended ceiling are designed to snap together at most joints, but there are situations where these pre-engineered joints do not apply. The most common place this occurs is at an outside wall where you must cut short pieces to abut the wall track. At these joints, there is no automatic way to lock the two tracks together, and sometimes it's fine to leave them unattached. However, to increase the stability of the track assembly, you can cut a small tab onto the end of the short track and use a pop rivet to fasten it to the wall track. A **pop-rivet gun** is a relatively inexpensive tool, and very easy to use. First, drill a small diameter hole through the two pieces you wish to join; insert the rivet into the gun; and push the nose through the holes in the two parts. Squeeze the handles on the gun repeatedly until the stem snaps off, locking the parts together. Pop rivets are available in a range of lengths, diameters, and materials, making the tool a versatile and useful addition to your general tool kit. You will find it valuable for joining sheet-metal assemblies, such as gutters and leaders, around the home and for automobile body repairs.

The wall tracks for a suspended ceiling need to be in-stalled along a level line around the perimeter of the room. You can use a spirit level to establish this line, but in a large room, there is considerable room for error when using a relatively short tool. As an alternative, you can rent a laser level from a tool rental center. This tool generates a continuous, level beam of light at whatever height you establish. Then, you can simply install the track with its edge aligned with the beam.

Acoustic ceiling tiles are also quite simple to install. In most cases, you will first fasten furring strips to the ceiling, 12 inches on center, across the entire room. Then you staple the tiles to the strips through the tongue that extends along two sides of each tile. Of course, you need a **staple gun** to do this. Any home center or hardware store will offer a fine selection of these guns. You will find manual models that rely on hand pressure to squeeze the lever that drives the staple, and you will find electric models, where you only need to pull a trigger; either type of stapler will be fine for this type of job. You only need to balance the relative ease of use of the electric gun against the inconvenience of having an extension cord attached to the tool.

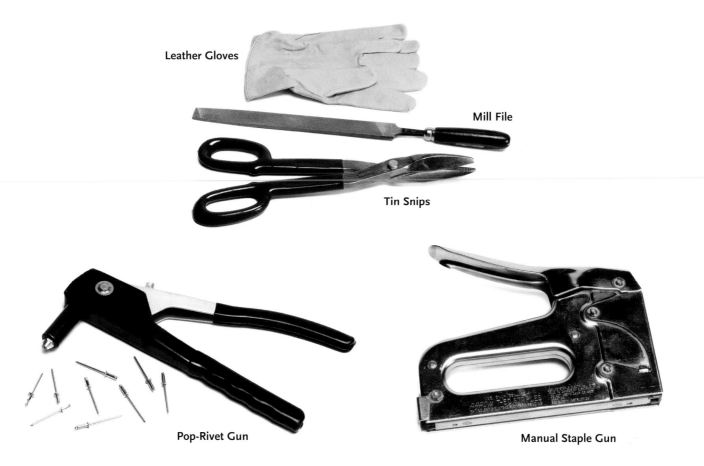

Leather Gloves

Mill File

Tin Snips

Pop-Rivet Gun

Manual Staple Gun

Tools for Drywall Soffits, Medallions, and Domes

Quite a few ceiling improvements involve some type of drywall work. If you are planning on adding a soffit or cove lighting structure that will be faced in drywall, it's obvious that your work will include a healthy dose of drywall finishing. But drywall repairs can occur as part of other projects as well, especially those that involve cutting into the existing ceiling or applying a decorative element to the ceiling surface. Even a project that is limited to applying paint or installing wallpaper can end up requiring some patching or repair of the ceiling surface.

If your job involves the installation of large drywall sheets to the ceiling, you should consider employing some mechanical help to get the sheets in place. You could simply entice a friend or family member to help you lift the sheets, but this is extremely awkward and entails a sub-stantial risk of injury, for you need to hold the sheet in place as you fasten it to the framing. For another option, you can build a "dead-man" frame to support the sheet, but this technique can make it difficult to accurately position the sheet. The wise alternative is to rent a drywall hoist from a tool rental center. With a **drywall hoist** you can install heavy sheets by yourself without any stress or strain. The tool is equipped with locking caster wheels so that it rolls easily but can be fixed in place when necessary, and a tilting table for easy loading. You then use the large hand wheel to raise the sheet against the ceiling joists or soffit framing, locking it into position so that you can install the screws or nails, completely eliminating anxiety or need to rush the process.

For drywall finishing you will need a set of

Drywall Hoist

taping knives and a **pan** to hold the drywall compound. Knives are offered in a range of sizes ranging in width from 3 inches to 14 inches. As you might expect, professional finishers each develop their own preference as to the size of knives they use, but in most cases, three knives of increasing size are used for the finish coats. For a homeowner approaching this job, a 5-inch knife is a good choice for applying the drywall tape and first coat of compound. Then, for the second and third coats, you can use 8-inch and 10-inch knives. Pans, also called "mudpans," look like oversized bread pans, and are available in both plastic and metal, and either material will serve you well. It is particularly important to thoroughly clean the tools and pan after each use, because even tiny dried bits

of compound can cause real problems in the finishing process.

Because you will be working on the ceiling, it is especially important that you get a **pole sander** for smoothing the finish coats. This assembly consists of a 3½ x 9-inch pad with a swiveling pole socket on its back side, and clips to hold either a **sanding screen** or sandpaper. Both screens and paper are sold in packages, or individually, precut to fit these sanders. You can purchase poles of various lengths, or use a broom handle as an extension—this system will allow you to sand the ceiling with your feet on the floor, rather than up on a ladder. Remember to always wear a suitable dust mask and eye protection when sanding drywall.

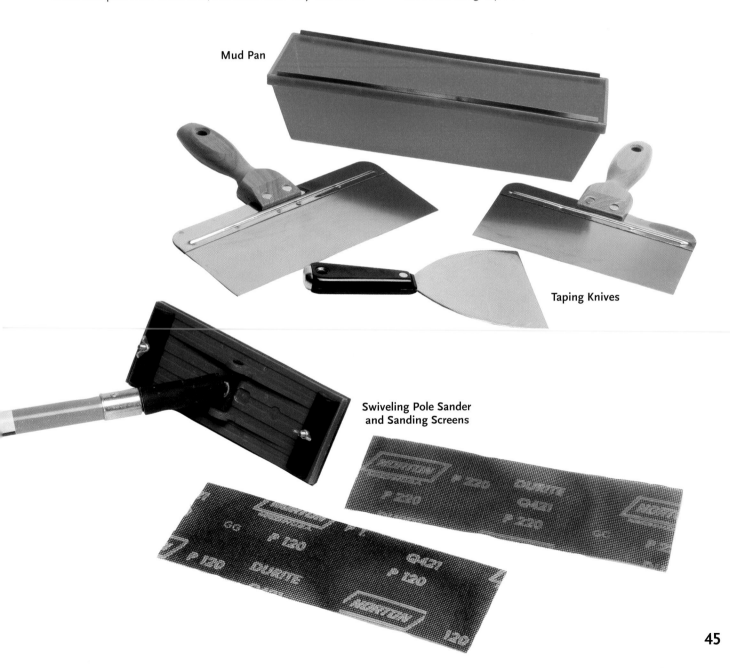

Mud Pan

Taping Knives

Swiveling Pole Sander
and Sanding Screens

TOOLS FOR CORNICES, WOOD BEAMS, COFFERS

Once you enter the world of cornices, wood beams, and coffered ceilings, you open the door to a pretty substantial realm of possible tool purchases. Because all of these improvements deal with carpentry techniques, most of the tools will have that orientation, but some will also have applications in other disciplines. You could easily use one of these projects as an excuse to equip your home shop, but it's not really necessary to have every possible tool to successfully complete most jobs. You'll certainly find that some jobs are made easier if you have a tool designed for that specific task, but there is usually an alternative approach that will provide equal results.

Coping Saw

When you plan to install wood cornice moldings as part of your ceiling improvement, you will need to master the process of cutting coped joints at inside corners. A coped joint is one in which the end of one of the intersecting pieces of molding is cut to fit the face profile of the opposite corner piece. Mastering this technique requires a bit of practice, but its use ensures tight, gap-free joints that will not open up over time, something that is not guaranteed when using an inside miter joint.

As you might expect, the primary tool for cutting these joints is called a coping saw. This tool has a "C"-shaped frame attached to a short wooden handle. A thin blade is held in tension between the ends of the frame. There are swivel fixtures at either end of the blade, allowing you to orient the blade in whatever direction is best to achieve the sharp turns necessary to follow the profile of complex molding. In addition, you have the ability to mount the blade so that it cuts on either the "pull" or "push" stroke, giving you even more options to control the cut.

Rasps and Files

While you will use a coping saw to cut the rough shape of a coped joint, it is almost always necessary to further refine the profile to create a tight fit. This can be accom-

Coping Saw

File Card

Files and Rasps

plished with a variety of tools, including knives and sandpaper. But the most useful tools for making fine adjustments to a coped profile are rasps and files. These abrasive tools are offered in a wide range of shapes, sizes, and tooth profiles. You will find some rasps that have a very aggressive cut and some files that leave an extremely smooth surface. Make your selection based on the requirements of your particular job—your collection will build over time, and you will certainly learn to appreciate the usefulness of these simple tools. To keep files and rasps working at maximum efficiency, purchase a file card to remove accumulated wood fibers from the teeth. The card features a surface of short, thin wires that you can use to brush away accumulated debris.

Angle Gauge and Sliding Adjustable Bevel

The most demanding part of a cornice installation is fitting the joints at inside and outside corners, and to do this properly, you first need to determine the exact angle of the corner. Even if a room is a square or rectangle, the actual corner angles may not be exactly 90 degrees as you would expect. Careless framing techniques, warped framing lumber, or the buildup of drywall compound can all cause these angles to vary. And there are plenty of situations where walls are intentionally built at angles other than 90 degrees, such as for bay windows. As a result, you need a way to measure the true wall angles, and that tool is the adjustable angle gauge. You can find many varieties of gauges but most have two legs that can be held against the two walls at a corner. You can then tighten a locking screw and remove the tool to read the resulting angle off a graduated scale. To cut a miter joint for that corner, you simply set the saw to make a cut equal to ½ of the total angle reading.

If you just need to copy an angle without taking a measurement, you can use an adjustable sliding bevel. This is a more compact tool than an angle gauge, and has the additional benefit of a sliding blade to accommodate a short corner. You will use this tool to directly transfer an angle to a piece of lumber or molding. Or you can also use it, in combination with a protractor or divider, for bisecting an angle. (See page 48.) Loosen the nut, and then hold the body of the gauge against one side of the angle. Allow the blade to rest against the opposite side of the angle and then tighten the nut to hold the setting.

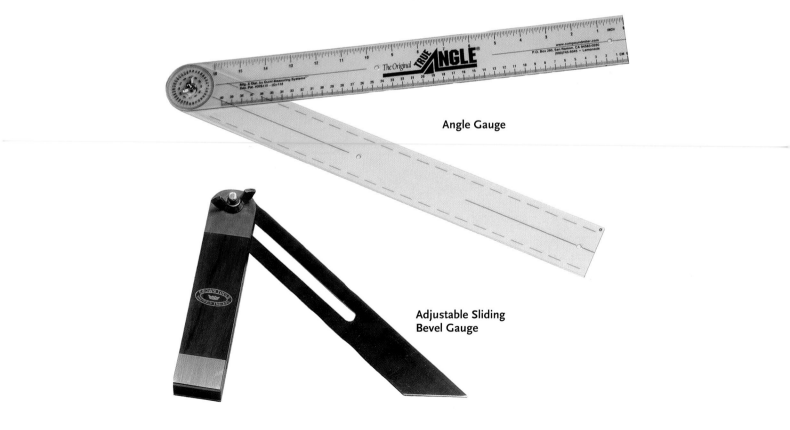

Angle Gauge

Adjustable Sliding Bevel Gauge

bisecting an angle

You can use geometry to determine the proper miter angle. Begin by taking a reading of the angle using an adjustable bevel gauge. Transfer the angle to a piece of scrap cardboard or plywood. Then use a set of dividers to mark out equal distances from the apex of the angle along each leg. Place the dividers on each of those marks and, using the same distance setting, make two intersecting arcs in the center of the angle. Draw a line from the apex of the angle through the intersecting point to indicate an angle that is one-half of the original. Use an angle gauge to measure the resulting angle.

1 To bisect the angle of an outside corner, use an adjustable sliding bevel gauge to copy the angle.

2 Transfer the corner angle to a piece of scrap plywood or cardboard.

3 Use a set of dividers to mark out equal distances from the apex of the angle down each leg.

4 Place the dividers on each of the previously established marks, and using the same setting, scribe two intersecting arcs in the center of the angle.

5 Draw a line that connects the apex of the angle with the intersection of the two arcs. This line divides the original angle into two equal parts.

6 Use an angle measuring gauge to determine the desired miter-saw setting.

Chisels

In many cornice or beam projects, you may find that you never need a chisel, but if you do need one, there is no good substitute. Chisels are the tool of choice for paring and fitting joints or cutting pieces to fit around an obstacle, such as an outlet, pipe, or light fixture. A basic set of butt chisels with four different sized blades, $1/4$-, $1/2$-, $3/4$-, and 1-inch, will serve you well for all around carpentry use. These tools can be guided by hand or struck with a hammer or mallet. For best performance and maximum safety, always keep the chisels razor sharp with a sharpening stone and honing guide, and store them with guards to protect the blades.

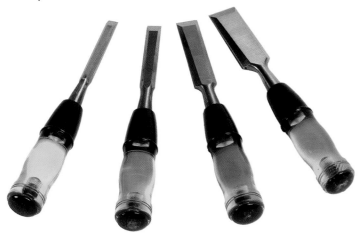

Chisels

Block Plane

When you first try to fit a piece of wooden trim against a ceiling or wall surface, it is often the case that some gaps will exist between the different materials. This situation is usually a result of hollows or bumps in the drywall or plaster, or it might be a consequence of bowed lumber. Regardless of the cause, your job is to create a tight joint between the parts, and the best tool for the job is often the block plane. Block planes feature a cutting iron that is about $1/2$ inches wide, mounted with its bevel facing up at a low-cutting angle. The body of the plane is quite short, about 6 inches in length, making it easy to hold in one hand. For best results with the plane, it is important that you keep the cutting iron razor sharp and, to that end, always fully retract the blade into the body of the plane before you put it away.

Clamps

There are times in most carpentry jobs where you just need an extra set of hands to hold or immobilize a part. And cornice or beamed ceiling projects are likely to be those types of jobs. Clamps are handy for applying pressure to parts during a glue-up assembly, but they are also valuable for temporarily holding parts in position while you drive nails or screws. You will also find them useful as a makeshift vise to hold a workpiece steady while you shape a joint or plane an edge. For a simple carpentry job, you should not need a large selection of clamps, but two or three small bar clamps or quick-action clamps will serve you well.

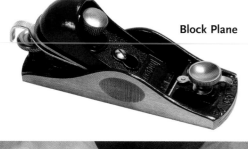

Block Plane

Spring Clamps

Small Bar Clamps

Table Saw

Given the generous selection of lumber sizes that most home centers offer, you can sometimes purchase material in the exact widths required for a job. But there are also projects that demand a more tailored approach, and in these situations you will need to rip the stock to size. While you can use a circular saw and rip guide for this task, you will inevitably find that you compromise efficiency and some safety by making that choice. This is particularly true when the ripping must yield stock of very narrow widths. The alternative lies in using a table saw for these cuts. Fortunately, many tool manufacturers now offer compact, portable table saws with 10-inch-diameter blades, and these can yield great results for a relatively modest investment. If you are planning to do some extensive work in your home shop, the table saw will certainly be the center of activity. All saws come equipped with blade guards and splitter/antikickback assemblies, and you should use definitely use them. Most models will also have both a miter gauge and rip fence as standard accessories. To protect your fingers, develop the habit of always using a push stick to guide narrow stock past the blade.

Miter Saw

For jobs that involve molding installation, cutting the joints at inside and outside corners is usually the most challenging part of the project. The tool you'll need for this is a miter saw. For the simplest projects—those that require only square and 45-degree miter cuts—you can likely get by with the most basic type of miter setup. For a very modest cash investment, you can purchase a wooden or plastic miter box with small backsaw that will make these elementary cuts. For more advanced jobs that demand some degree of flexibility in the angle of cut, you will find many different options, beginning with an adjustable hand miter saw and including simple power miter saws and sliding compound miter saws. As you might expect, as the features of the different models increase, the cost of the tool increases proportionately; at the high end, you will find saws for professional use that cost over $600.

Table Saw

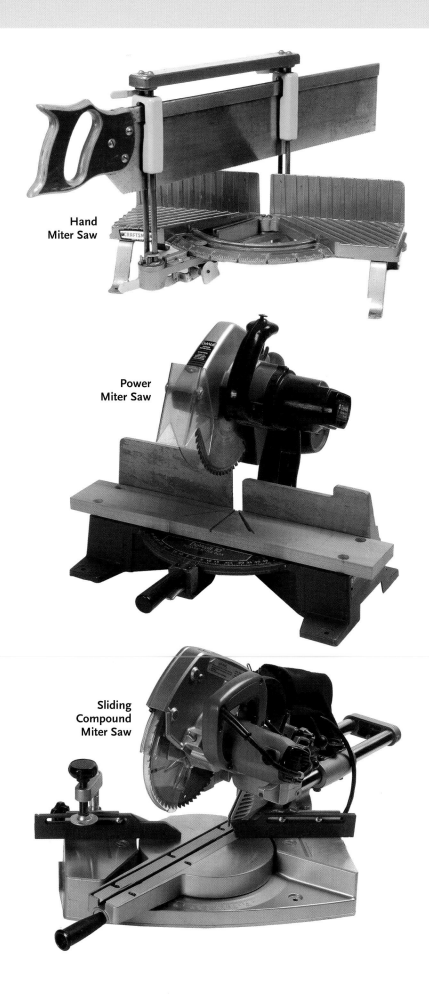

Hand Miter Saw

Power Miter Saw

Sliding Compound Miter Saw

Saber Saw

A saber saw, also called a portable jigsaw, can be a valuable addition to your tool collection. If a job calls for curved or circular cuts, this is the tool for the job; but you will also find that it can stand in for a circular saw as well, making straight cuts in either solid wood or plywood. These saws accept a wide range of blades for cutting wood, plastics, and metal. Most models have a tilting base for bevel cuts and a switch that allows you to select either a reciprocating or orbital motion for the blade. You will also find some very useful accessories offered for this type of saw, some offered by the manufacturer and others as after-market options; these include a rip guide, circle cutting jig, and coping foot (for cutting inside corner joints on moldings).

Saber Saw

Router

A router is one of the most versatile tools in the wood-workers' arsenal. Consisting of a vertically mounted motor with a tool-holding collet on its bottom end, the router can be used to produce moldings, shape edges, cut grooves, and duplicate uniquely shaped parts from templates. For ceiling projects, the most likely use for a router will be in making your own moldings or in modifying stock lumber for use in beams or cornices by cutting rabbets and dadoes. You will find routers in a range of sizes and power ratings. The smallest models are used for delicate trim work, and the largest machines, rated at 3 hp or more, are used as production tools in industry. For most home-related jobs, however, you will find a router with a motor rating of $1\frac{1}{2}$ or $1\frac{3}{4}$ hp to be perfect.

Router

Routers are offered in two basic configurations—those with a fixed base and those with a plunge base. With a fixed-base model, you need to set the depth of cut before turning on the machine, usually by setting an adjusting ring on the base and turning a locking screw. A plunge-base router allows you to lower the spinning bit into the workpiece; there are normally a series of adjustable depth stops that you can preset to limit the depth of cut. Plunge-base routers are considered to be more flexible in general use, but if your primary purpose is to make moldings or cut shaped edges on panel stock, the fixed-base option will be fine.

Most router bits are equipped with a shaft that measures either $\frac{1}{4}$ or $\frac{1}{2}$ inch in diameter. Some routers will accept different collets to hold either size bit, but some models are equipped with only a $\frac{1}{4}$-inch collet—these are typically meant to be used on light-duty jobs. Consider this feature carefully when purchasing a tool, as the selection of bits for molding work is heavily weighted to those with $\frac{1}{2}$-inch shanks.

Some routers are sold as part of a kit that includes a carrying case and edge guide. But if your particular router does not come with a guide, you should consider purchasing one, as it is an extremely handy accessory. While many edge-shaping bits are equipped with a ball-bearing pilot guide, there are also many bits that come without this feature; an edge guide allows you the flexibility of using any type of bit and modifying the depth of cut of those that have a pilot. In addition, the guide can be useful for cutting grooves parallel with the edge of a board or panel.

Plate Joiner

Ceiling projects that involve building beams or coffers will require you to carefully position and join many parts to yield the structural components of the ceiling. Sometimes, you can use nails or screws to assemble these parts, but in other situations, you need fasteners that are not visible. While there are many types of joints used in woodworking, quite a few of these options would require you to devote considerable time and effort in their mastery, a pursuit far from that of improving your ceiling. Fortunately, the plate joiner provides a simple and strong method of joining two wood parts, and this system doesn't require months of practice to master.

The plate joiner has a small spinning blade that you advance into the wood to a preset depth, corresponding to one of three different-sized plates. The joining plates are football-shaped wafers of compressed wood, about $\frac{1}{8}$

● ROUTER TABLE

While the router is a powerful and flexible tool, you will find that some jobs, like shaping narrow stock, can be awkward and a bit dangerous with a handheld router. Fortunately there is a simple and convenient alternative approach for these tasks—mounting the router upside down in a router table. You will find commercial models sold in home centers and specialty woodworking tool supply houses, some tabletop models and others that have freestanding bases. The basic design has a router base mounted on the bottom of a flat table-like surface with a hole for the cutting bit. You mount the router in the table; adjust the height of the bit; clamp a fence to the table; and push the wood stock past the spinning bit. Because the bit is exposed, you also need to take added precautions for safety. Commercial tables offer a guard to cover the bit and often have provision for hold-down jigs to keep the stock against the table and fence; you should always use these safety accessories, as they protect your hands from injury and promote a better-quality cut.

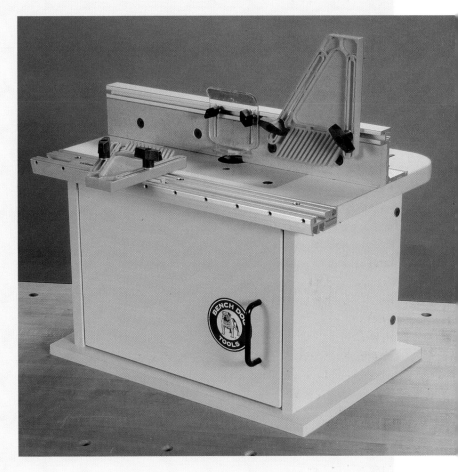

inch thick. You cut matching semicircular slots in the mating board faces; apply glue to the slots and to both faces of the plate; then insert the plate into the slot and assemble the parts. Normally, it is recommended that you clamp the parts for at least 15 minutes to allow the moisture in the glue to cause the plates to expand.

Joining plates have become one of the most widely used joining methods in the woodworking trades, due to the speed, convenience, and strength of the system. Even if parts will be fastened with nails or screws, it is sometimes useful to install joining plates as a method of locating the parts in relation to one another. For this type of use, you don't need to apply glue to either the slots or plates, further simplifying the assembly process.

Plate Joiner

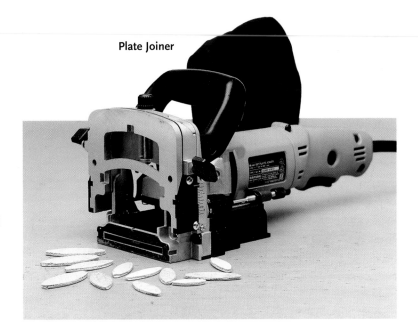

Nail Guns and Compressor

For most carpentry projects, including beams, cornices, and coffers, that qualify as ceiling improvements, nails are the primary means of fastening the components together and to the wall or ceiling structure. While it is perfectly fine to use a hammer to drive those nails, there is also good reason to consider the use of a pneumatic nail gun. First, continued pounding with a hammer can sometimes result in cracks in a plaster or drywall surface. Because a hand-driven nail often requires several solid blows to drive it home, the cumulative impact is considerable over the course of a job. In comparison, a pneumatic gun will drive any nail with one blow, in any type of wood. When driving nails by hand into hardwood, it is necessary to drill a small pilot hole for each nail to prevent the wood from splitting or the nail from bending. A nail gun will easily drive the nails through hardwoods, softwoods, or even MDF, without splitting and with no need for pilot holes. With traditional finishing nails, the diameter of the fastener increases as the nails get longer, but gun nails are designed to be of uniform diameter regardless of their length, leaving a smaller hole to fill. Finally, hand nailing requires two hands—one hand to hold the nail and another to swing the hammer—and this can make it hard to support a piece of molding or lumber. Using a nail gun requires only one hand, and this leaves your free hand available to adjust the position of the piece being fastened.

Guns are divided into two main categories—those that drive 15- or 16-gauge fasteners are called nail guns, and those that drive thinner, 18-gauge brads are called brad guns. Typically gun nails are used for most substantial fastening jobs, while brads are used for thin, delicate moldings.

Using a nail gun requires a compressor to provide air pressure to drive the nails. Compact models are available with motors rated between $3/4$ and $2 1/2$ hp in both oil-less and oil-lubricated designs; either type is fine for driving a finishing nailer. You will also need an air hose to connect the compressor to the gun. For light-duty interior work a $1/4$-inch-diameter x 25-foot hose is sufficient.

Brad Gun and Nail Gun

Compressor

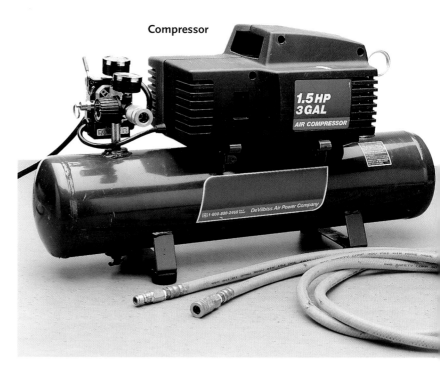

USING A NAIL OR BRAD GUN

1 Load nails into the gun magazine by sliding them through an opening at the back end of the gun. Release the spring catch that applies pressure to the back side of the nail clip.

2 Hold the gun perpendicular to the face of the molding, and press the safety release at the nose of the gun against the wood surface. Pull the trigger to drive the nail.

3 To load brads, open the magazine by releasing the locking lever and pulling back on the cover. Lay the brads in the gun, and slide the cover forward until it clicks shut.

4 You can adjust the countersink depth on both nail and brad guns by turning a knurled wheel behind the nose of the gun.

Sanders

An important, though generally unpopular, part of any woodworking project is sanding. Sanding is the process that takes the raw materials and prepares them to accept a clear or painted finish. Even though most wood products seem to have a relatively smooth surface when you purchase them, in fact, most of these items have mill marks, scratches, and dirt that need to be removed before you apply paint, stain, or varnish. Of course, sanding is a messy business, raising dust that can be irritating to eyes and lungs, and it is not particularly exciting. But with the proper tools, you can speed the process and ensure great results, providing you with a finished project that you can point to with pride.

There are many jobs where a sanding strategy will make your job much easier. This usually means that you sand individual parts before assembly, leaving only a light touch-up to be done immediately before applying the finish. The way that you institute this idea will depend on the particulars of the job, but remember to consider the logistics of sanding when planning the steps of your project. Regardless of the sanding tools you use or the timing of the sanding, remember to always wear a proper dust mask and goggles for protection.

The simplest sanding tool is a block of wood around which you can wrap a piece of sandpaper. This is the method of choice for overall sanding of small jobs or for easing the sharp edges of any wood assembly. You can use as the block any type of wood that you have available, cutting it to an appropriate size for your particular job. If you want a commercial version, you will find blocks of cork and rubber, some that offer clips or slots to hold the sandpaper in place. For sanding moldings, you might need to use a bit of imagination in selecting an appropriate backer—often a dowel, pencil, or small cardboard tube can be used as a sanding block.

For large projects, you will inevitably want some mechanical help to speed the sanding process. Power sanders are available in a number of styles, each with its own advantages. For aggressive smoothing of rough surfaces, a small belt sander is very useful. Most accept a 3- or 4-inch-wide belt in a range of grits from very coarse (40 grit) to very fine (220 grit). When using a belt sander, it is extremely important that you keep the tool moving

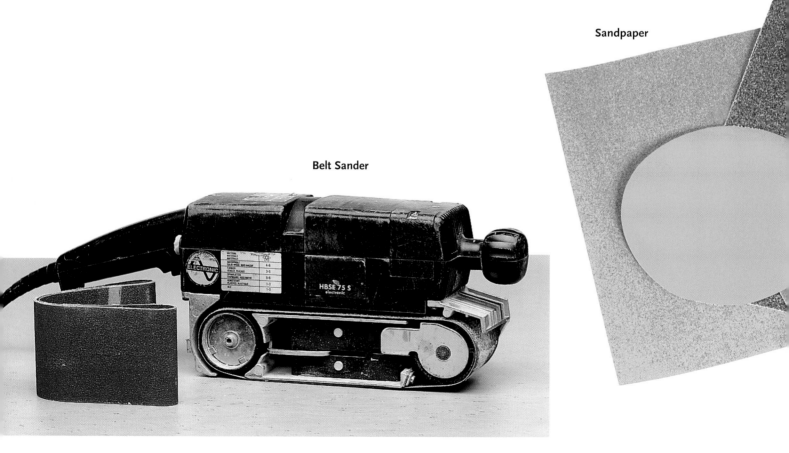

Sandpaper

Belt Sander

parallel with the grain at all times, because resting it in one position can cause a deep gouge that is difficult to repair.

Finish sanding is usually accomplished by using a vibrating pad sander. These are available in $\frac{1}{4}$- and $\frac{1}{2}$-sheet sizes (a full sheet of sandpaper measures 9 x 11 inches) and are usually the least expensive type of sander. You will find that these pad sanders are the best choice for jobs that require vertical or upside-down sanding, as they are quite light and easy to control.

A random-orbital sander is a finish sander with a disc-shaped pad. The pad turns on an eccentric spindle so that it creates very tiny swirl marks on the wood surface. This type of sander has the advantage of being quite aggressive in removal of stock while leaving a fine finish, but it is somewhat awkward to use in a vertical position. You will find these an excellent choice for jobs that can be sanded flat on the workbench before installation. Random-orbital sanders are provided with two types of pads for sandpaper mounting—a plain rubber pad will accept discs with a pressure-sensitive adhesive, and a hook-and-loop pad will accept discs with a hook-and-loop backer.

smart tip

SAFETY CONSIDERATIONS

WORKING ON A CEILING TREATMENT MEANS YOU WILL SPEND MUCH TIME CLIMBING UP AND DOWN LADDERS OR SCAFFOLDING, SO IT PAYS TO USE STURDY, WELL-MADE EQUIPMENT. MANY OF THE PROJECTS CALL FOR USING POWER SAWS. YOU SHOULD FOLLOW THE MANUFACTURER'S OPERATING INSTRUCTIONS AND FOLLOW THE RULES FOR SAFE OPERATION. GUARD AGAINST INJURY BY WEARING SAFETY GOGGLES AND, IN SOME SITUATIONS, A DUST MASK OR RESPIRATOR. A GOOD PAIR OF WORK GLOVES IS A MUST FOR SANDING AND FINISHING WORK AND FOR INSTALLING TIN CEILINGS. AS WITH ANY PROJECT, PROVIDE AN OPEN WORKSPACE FOR YOURSELF, AND MAKE SURE THERE IS PLENTY OF LIGHT ON THE JOB AT HAND.

Orbital Sanders

60 SOLID-COLOR CEILINGS

60 BORDERS

62 CREATING LINEAR BORDERS

64 CREATING REPEATING PATTERN BORDERS

66 CREATING STENCIL BORDERS

3 paint techniques

For someone who has little experience in hands-on home improvements, those projects that involve paint are clearly the least intimidating. Even if you think of yourself as someone lacking in artistic ability, you can still tackle a painting project and have great results. There is almost no limit to the ways you can use paint to enliven and transform a room. The projects in this chapter involve using stencils to decorate the perimeter of a ceiling. As you will see, you have the choice of creating your own unique design or purchasing a premade stencil.

SOLID-COLOR CEILINGS

Probably the easiest ceiling upgrade is to just paint the ceiling a color other than white—the simplest approach is to use a shade of the wall color. Or you can select a color that complements the color of the walls, perhaps a color already featured in a wall covering, window treatment, or piece of artwork, or furniture. Ceiling color has a definite effect on the way we experience a room; lighter colors tend to make the room seem taller, and darker colors create a more closed-in feeling. As a general rule, if you want to create the sense of a higher ceiling, use paint that is at least a shade or two lighter than the wall color, and if you want to make the ceiling seem lower, use paint a shade or two darker than the walls.

You can play with this perception using two other simple variations: carry the ceiling color down onto the walls by 12 or 14 inches, or conversely, bring the color of the walls up onto the ceiling surface, creating a solid border. Either of these techniques can be further embellished by applying a wood molding at the junction of the contrasting colors.

Keep in mind that the sheen of the paint you use will also have an effect on the atmosphere in the room. While it's most common to use flat paint on the ceiling, a dark space can sometimes benefit from the use of a finish with a higher gloss that will reflect more light. Because high-gloss paint will tend to emphasize any defects or uneven areas in the ceiling surface, you might consider using paint with an eggshell or satin finish instead—this will still provide additional reflectivity to brighten a dark room.

BORDERS

Regardless of the ceiling color, you can make a strong design statement by painting a linear, textural, or figurative border along the edge of the ceiling.

And depending on the type of border upon which you finally decide, there are a variety of ways that you can transfer the idea to your ceiling. Because the universe of potential border patterns is so vast, an entire book could easily be devoted to a presentation of the options. However, as an introduction to the concept, you can consider the three border techniques on the following pages.

While the techniques required for a painted border are not complex, any type of work on the ceiling will be physically demanding. Plan your work so that you have access to a stable stepladder, or construct a scaffold that places you in at a comfortable height for painting the design. It can take several hours to execute even a simple design, so it is often best to divide the project into manageable portions to minimize aches and pains in neck and shoulders.

● REPAIRING MINOR CEILING DEFECTS

Before you begin a paint job, take a few minutes to inspect the condition of the ceiling, looking for subtle cracks or holes that need repair. These minor defects are more likely to show when the ceiling is painted a color other than white, so the effort to repair them will help to ensure a professional-quality job. Of course, if there are serious structural problems, such as badly cracked or sagging plaster, more drastic repairs, or even total replacement of the ceiling, could be required.

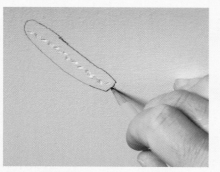

Use a flashlight or portable work light to help locate spots that need attention. Because these areas can sometimes be hard to see, lightly outline each defect with a pencil mark.

Use putty or drywall joint compound to fill the cracks or holes. Apply the filler using a putty knife that is at least 1-inch wider than the defect, and allow the filling material to dry completely before sanding it level with the surrounding surface.

A ceiling color that matches the wall makes the room feel more intimate.

CREATING LINEAR BORDERS

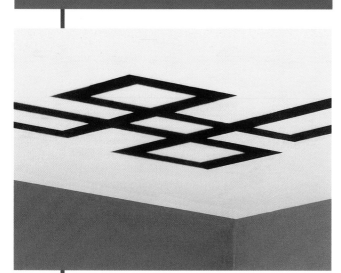

project

A linear border can bring a sense of elegance and formality to a room. And by creating a decorative focal point in each corner, as the border changes direction, you can add another dimension to the treatment. A border can be as simple as a single line that runs parallel with the wall; it could be as narrow as $3/4$ inch or as wide as several inches. Or you might run two, three, or four parallel lines around the perimeter of the room, creating a design that really draws the eye and makes a strong statement. In addition to the basic form you choose, you have the option of bringing some color to the design, as well. It's always safe to use the main wall color as a border, but you could also use an accent color or metallic paint to create a more energetic feel. When the border includes multiple lines, consider using two or more colors.

TOOLS & MATERIALS
▌ Graph paper
▌ Foam board
▌ Utility knife
▌ Straightedge
▌ Painter's tape
▌ Paint
▌ $1\frac{1}{2}$-in.-wide paintbrush

1 It's always a good idea to make a scale drawing of your border design before committing it to your ceiling. Use graph paper to sketch the pattern, including the distance between the wall and the border. Graph paper provides an easy way to lay out the design—you can try out several versions of your idea, and decide which works best, without the risk of wasting time and money on a concept you won't like.

4 Hold the pattern against the ceiling at a corner, with the two outer edges of the foam board against the walls—this will properly locate the jig. Next, use a sharp pencil to place reference marks to indicate the intersecting lines of the design.

2 When your border includes an intricate corner design, you can save a lot of time by constructing a simple layout jig from foam-core board (available at art and craft supply stores). Begin by cutting a square piece of the board that is large enough to accommodate the design and extend to the walls at the room's corners. Then use a large square and felt-tipped marker to transfer the pattern from your scale drawing.

3 Place the foam board on another piece of scrap foam or heavy cardboard; then use a sharp utility knife to cut out a window at each inside and outside corner intersection. This will allow the pattern to maintain its shape while still providing you with a way to mark the critical points on the ceiling.

5 Use a ruler or straightedge to connect the reference points to complete the corner design. At the ends of the corner pattern, you can use a long straightedge to extend the lines, parallel with the wall, connecting with the design in the opposite corners of the room.

6 Apply painter's masking tape to the ceiling to outline the border pattern. Carefully place the tape so that it sits just outside the pencil lines—this will allow you to cover the pencil lines with paint, leaving a clean edge. A 1½-in.-wide bristle brush is ideal for painting the border on the ceiling. Use a relatively dry brush to minimize paint drips—it's easier to apply two light coats than to clean up a messy application.

CREATING REPEATING PATTERN BORDERS

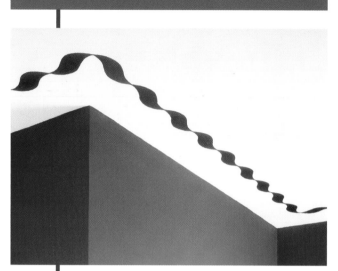

project

1 Once you have arrived at a desired pattern, transfer the design, in the final size, to a piece of heavy cardboard. Use a pair of sharp scissors to cut out the template, cutting just to the outside of the layout lines. If necessary, use a piece of coarse sandpaper or a small file to refine the shape and smooth the edges.

To extend your border options, you can take a simple pattern—either your own design or something borrowed from another source—and repeat it down the length of the ceiling. Further personalize the border by varying the spacing between the repeating elements of the design or by using different painting techniques or materials. In the example shown in the photo sequence, a simple free-hand form is linked end-to-end to create an undulating ribbon pattern; a bronze-toned metallic paint allows the design to catch and reflect light, creating an eye-catching contrast with the deep-colored walls of the room.

While this border places the design elements adjacent to one another, keep in mind that you can also allow spaces within the border. The best approach when developing a plan is to make a scale drawing of potential designs on graph paper so that you can better judge the eventual appearance. Don't hesitate to explore variations of your initial concept. Ideas can develop as you consider different options, and your ultimate solution may be something completely unique and unexpected.

The pattern used here is 5 inches long. But if you find that the 5-inch repeating interval does not work for the length of your walls, you can redraw the design either larger or smaller to yield a size that suits your room. Because there are often walls of varying size in a room, you may need to adjust the pattern from one wall to another; small variations in length will not be easily detected on different walls.

Determine the overall border dimension for each wall by subtracting twice the distance of the border to the walls from the length of each wall. For example, if the wall is 129 inches long and the center of your border will be 5 inches from the wall, subtract 10 (2 x 5 inches) from 129 to yield 119. Next, divide that length by the number of repeated patterns you wish to use (in this case 25): $119 \div 25 = 4.76$. For practical purposes, you can round off this dimension to $4^3/_4$ inches, so you would simply reduce the length of your pattern to that dimension.

TOOLS & MATERIALS
▌ Graph paper
▌ Scissors
▌ Folding ruler
▌ Straightedge
▌ Paint
▌ Paintbrush or artist brush

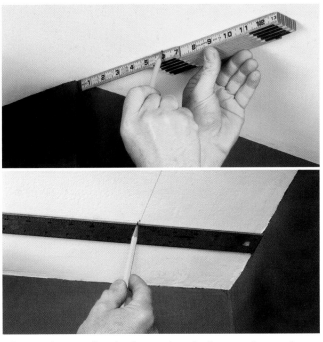

2 The border shown in the photos was created using a metallic bronze acrylic paint. This kind of paint is readily available at art supply or craft stores. It is compatible with latex paint, and cleanup is simple—just wash hands and brushes with soap and water. Select appropriate brushes that will work well with your design.

3 Begin your border layout by placing marks on the ceiling to indicate the centerline of the design (top). In this example, the border will be centered on a line 6 in. from the wall. Place marks at intervals of 2 or 3 ft. around the room, depending on the length of straight-edge you have available. Connect the layout marks (bottom).

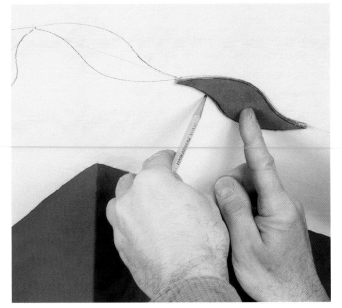

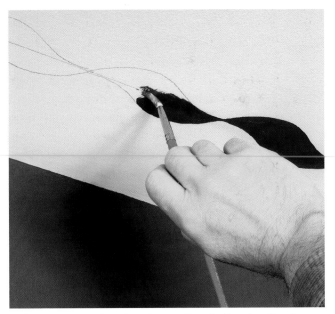

4 Beginning at an inside or outside corner, align one end of your pattern on the intersecting lines, and adjust its opposite end so that it rests directly on the layout line. Hold it in place while you trace around it with a sharp pencil. Move it to the next position down the line, and repeat the process. Whenever you turn a corner, you will need to flip the pattern over to create a mirror image of the design.

5 Use your artist's brush to paint the border. For the neatest job, just cover the pencil marks with paint so that you do not need to worry about erasing the lines after the paint dries. The metallic paint shown is quite thick, so it covers in a single coat.

CREATING STENCIL BORDERS

project

Most people are familiar with the use of stencils to create designs on walls, floors, and furniture. The same technique can be applied to a ceiling border, allowing you to draw on a vast library of available patterns or even to create your own design. The selection of commercially sold stencils is often categorized by theme, as many designs are related to a particular style or area of interest. For instance, you might find a group of stencils that reflect a musical motif, or others that refer to sports, images from nature, children's literature, or a specific architectural tradition. You will find stencils in arts-and-crafts supply houses, but for the largest selection, you should browse the many suppliers listed on the Internet. (See Resource Guide, page 180.)

Most commercially available stencils are made of Mylar or vinyl and are quite durable. Some patterns require only one stencil, but more complex designs—especially those that use multiple colors—might demand that you use two or three stencils, each representing a distinct part of the overall image. Stencils are often designed to be used in groups or in series, so it is common practice to include small registration marks that are used to accurately position them in relation to one another. In most cases, small triangular cutouts are located in the four corners of each stencil; after positioning a stencil, use a soft pencil to mark through the cutouts onto the ceiling surface. Then, when positioning the next stencil, align the registration cutouts with your previously marked triangles. If you do not want to place marks directly on the ceiling surface, you can place small pieces of painter's tape under the cutouts and draw the marks on them.

Some stencil designs are clearly meant to be a single color while others are more complex and are intended to feature multiple colors. In many cases, multi-color designs are those that include more than one stencil, each stencil representing a particularly colored part of the design. But if the design is large enough, specifically if there is adequate space between adjacent openings in the stencil, you can use multiple colors in even a single-stencil pattern. It is also possible to bring multiple techniques to any stencil design, using shading or outlining to enhance even a simple motif.

When it comes to applying paint to a stencil, you have a variety of tools and techniques you can employ. Stencil brushes are the most commonly used tools for painting stencils. These brushes come in a variety of sizes, but they are typically short-bristled, with bristles of approximately the same length; foam brushes are also available. With a stencil brush, you can use either a stippling technique, which involves tapping the end of the brush against the stencil opening, or a swirling technique, in which you move the brush in a circular motion. By combining these different methods and changing the pressure you use to apply the paint, you can create interesting variations in the pattern.

If your design demands a uniform application of a single color, you can use a small foam roller to apply the paint. Or you can experiment with a variety of different applicators to create unusual effects—small sponges, cotton balls, rags, and paper towels are only a few of the possible materials you might use. In most cases, it is a good idea to practice your application technique on some scrap cardboard or drywall before committing your design to the ceiling.

TOOLS & MATERIALS
- Stencil
- Spray adhesive
- Painter's tape
- Paint or liquid acrylics for stencils
- Stencil brush

1 When stenciling a border, it is important that the stencil be firmly adhered to the ceiling surface so that paint doesn't spread beyond the borders of the openings. One way to help ensure a good seal is to apply a light coat of artist's spray adhesive to the back surface of the stencil. This type of adhesive will help to hold the stencil in place, but the bond is temporary, and the stencil will be easy to remove and reposition. In general, the adhesive will remain viable for several applications of the stencil.

2 Place light pencil marks on the ceiling to indicate the outer edge of the stencil for its first placement. At an outside corner, allow the end point of the pattern to extend past the corner the same distance as that of the centerline of the pattern from the parallel wall—in the photo this distance was 3$\frac{1}{2}$ in. *(continued on page 68)*

(continued from page 67)

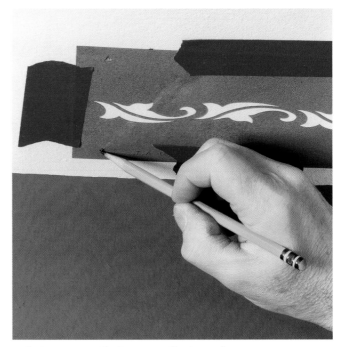

3 Place short strips of painter's tape along the edges of the stencil to ensure that it does not move while you apply the paint. If you use a low-tack tape, it will be easy to remove without causing any damage to the painted ceiling.

4 Most stencils have small triangular cutouts to serve as registration marks for repositioning the stencil to extend the border or to position a second overlay when applying more than one color to a design. Use a soft pencil to completely fill in each triangle to provide an accurate mark.

7 Remove excess paint from your brush by wiping it on an absorbent paper towel. It's important that your brush not carry excess paint—if you lightly wipe the brush across the back of your hand, it should not leave any paint behind.

8 Apply paint to the stencil openings using whatever technique you'd like, stippling or swirling, to create the desired effect. Take care to work paint into the corners of the pattern so that you have crisp edges. When you finish painting all openings in the stencil, carefully remove the tape, and gently lift the stencil away from the ceiling. Before repositioning the stencil, examine the top to make sure that no paint has bled onto that surface.

5 Although you can use a variety of paints to color a stencil, the most-common and easiest-to-use choices are liquid acrylics or stencil cremes. Either type of paint can be used just as it comes from its packaging. Stencil cremes are formulated to be dense and waxy, while liquid acrylics are the consistency of thick, heavy cream.

6 To use liquid acrylic paint, pour a small amount on a plate or plastic lid; then dab your stencil brush into the paint. In painting a stencil, you always want a dry brush, so use only the tip of the brush and do not overload it with paint.

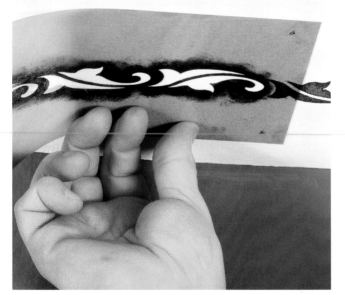

9 Use the triangular registration marks as a guide in positioning the stencil for the continuation of the border pattern. The pencil marks should completely fill the openings to ensure accurate placement. Once again, use strips of tape to keep the stencil from shifting position while you paint.

10 Finished stencil border.

72   DESIGN OPTIONS

75   INSTALLING A BORDER

4 wallpaper

It's not surprising that many people think of wallpaper as strictly a wall covering—considering that the name supports that notion—but ceiling decoration has also been a traditional use of this material, and the effects you can achieve with it can range from simple and austere to dazzling and majestic. If you're searching for a way to add color, texture, or graphic patterns to your ceiling, wallpaper may be the perfect solution. Perhaps you wish to create a room that evokes a particular historical period, particularly one of the predominant architectural genres that date to the mid-nineteenth century. You can easily find a selection of wallpapers that reflect these styles. Victorian, Arts and Crafts, Art Nouveau, and Art Deco patterns are all readily available, in addition to more-modern design themes that have evolved since the mid 1900s.

DESIGN OPTIONS

Wallpapers can bring a tremendous assortment of complex patterns, rich colors, and stunning optical effects to a room; they can be used on both walls and ceiling, or on the ceiling alone, in combination with painted or paneled wall treatments. You can use a single paper design to cover an entire ceiling or a combination of complementary patterns and colors to create an elaborate design of borders, panels, and medallions; or you can simply apply a wallpaper border as an accent on a plain painted ceiling.

■ **Types of Wallpaper.** In its most common form, wallpaper consists of machine-printed patterns on paper. But a simple search through the available materials will yield wall coverings that feature hand-screened patterns, grasscloth, woven fibers, metallic finishes, embossed linoleum, vinyl, and leather, each able to convey a particular spirit and design sensibility. Printed papers can display floral or other illustrative themes, pure geometric designs, or stylized decorative patterns. Grass and reed cloths might offer patterns that run either across the width of the roll or parallel with its length, with a variety of textures ranging from very fine to coarse or shaggy. Heavily embossed coverings made of linoleum or vinyl can suggest an elaborate plaster motif, while a metallic or leather covering can create a mood that's both exotic and intimate.

The installation of a basic wallpaper border is certainly not beyond the capabilities of an enthusiastic, handy homeowner. Of course, the laws of gravity make applying paper to a ceiling more challenging than hanging it on a wall. But once you develop a working technique, you will be surprised at how approachable this job can be. For a more elaborate project covering an entire ceiling—one that involves precise matching of patterns, multiple papers, or expensive hand-made or specialty coverings—seek professional installation if you don't have extensive experience.

Estimating Borders

If your project is confined to a border, material estimation is quite simple. Border papers typically come in narrow rolls 5 yards long (or 5 meters for imported papers), with the roll exactly as wide as the finished border. You will also find some patterns that are printed in multiples on a wide roll, requiring you to cut them apart before installation; this is particularly true of expensive hand-printed papers with specialty designs.

Measure the total length of the walls in your room, and then add a minimum of 15 to 20 percent to allow for waste and pattern matching. It is always a good idea to have some extra paper left over at the end of a job in case you need the material for future repairs, so you might consider purchasing a full extra roll as insurance.

For those jobs that entail covering an entire ceiling, especially if more than one pattern is to be used, you should take careful room measurements and consult with your wallpaper supplier to determine the amount you will need. Each paper has a different waste requirement, depending on the design and frequency of repeating patterns, so no universal guidelines will cover all materials and situations.

■ **Preparing the Room.** Although it's not particularly difficult to install a wallpaper border, your job will be easier if you prepare the room before you begin. Remove as much of the furniture from the room as possible, and if

● WALLPAPER ADHESIVE

Select a wallpaper adhesive that is compatible with the paper you are using. You will find adhesives that are specifically designed for border applications, and these are particularly useful because they provide extended open times. In general, wallpaper pastes are water based, so cleanup is easy. The consistency of the adhesive is thick and creamy, allowing you to spread it easily without any risk of tearing the paper. In addition, wallpaper paste is quite forgiving in that it allows you to slide the paper into place or peel it away from the surface to remove waste off-cuts and then reposition it for a tight joint.

You will also find some wallpaper that comes prepasted—these are products that are designed for D-I-Y installations. To activate the adhesive, you soak the paper in a water tray before installing it. This is a perfectly acceptable system, but it can also be pretty messy. So if you are not happy with the soaking technique, you can install prepasted paper using traditional adhesive; simply treat it as though it was unpasted paper.

An unusual wallpapering technique calls for running paper installed on walls up onto the ceiling.

you cannot completely empty the space, clear a path around the perimeter of the room by moving everything to the center. If you have paintings, photographs, or other hanging objects on the walls, it is also a good idea to remove them, as they are particularly vulnerable to being bumped by a stray elbow or damaged by dropped tools. Protect floors or carpets with drop cloths. It's not necessary to provide enough cloths to cover the entire room perimeter; simply have enough to cover a path along the longest wall in the room, moving them when each wall is complete.

■ **Job Logistics.** Installing wallpaper presents its own challenges, and working overhead just adds another level of complexity to the job. Although it is possible to install a border by yourself, you'll find it helpful to have an assistant to support the paper while you position it on the ceiling and smooth out bubbles and wrinkles.

To reach the ceiling, you can either use a pair of stepladders or, for better access, construct a scaffold to provide a continuous platform on which to work. The support for your scaffold can be a pair of low sawhorses or benches that you nail together from framing lumber. They should be strong and stable—you don't want to be worried about the safety of your work platform while you should be concentrating on the installation. Plan the

height of the scaffold so that you will be able to comfortably place your hands on the ceiling without stretching. For the scaffold boards, use 2x12 planks, available at any home center or lumberyard; clamp or nail the planks to the supports to maximize the stability of the platform. If you don't want to build your own scaffold, you can rent portable units from a tool-rental store. Most companies will offer supports and planks in a range of sizes at a reasonable cost.

■ **Preparing the Ceiling.** It's important to properly prepare your ceiling for a wallpaper border installation. As you might expect, this will help to ensure that the job looks great, but it will also make removal of the paper easier if you ever wish to redecorate. Preparing a surface for wallpaper is much the same as paint prep. Begin by inspecting the ceiling for holes or cracks, and fill them with putty, patching plaster, or drywall joint compound. Use a putty knife to remove any loose or peeling paint, and dull a gloss-painted surface by lightly sanding with 40- or 60-grit sandpaper; then vacuum the ceiling to remove any residual dust. Prime and paint the entire ceiling carefully following the paint manufacturer's instructions—a 100-percent-acrylic paint is generally the best choice. Allow the finish coat of paint to dry for at least 48 hours before applying the border.

Although mostly used on walls, borders have a distinctive look when used on ceilings.

INSTALLING A BORDER

For a simple rectangular room with only inside corners, begin by cutting the border paper to lengths slightly longer than each of the walls—2 to 4 inches extra is sufficient. When planning your cuts, examine the patterns on the paper to determine whether it is necessary to match the pattern on adjacent walls. Corners generally receive mitered cuts to allow the pattern to remain continuous from one wall to the next, and these are always cut in place after the border is installed. Some papers have uniform designs that can be seamed without considering a match. If your pattern requires matching, try to anticipate your cuts so that the figure is symmetrical on both sides of an inside corner. But because wall length can vary, this may not always be possible; you may need to decide which corners are the most likely to draw attention and locate the best matches there.

If your room has one or more outside corners, you should begin your layout at those points. Because an outside corner projects into the room, it typically draws the eye and will be a focal point of the decorative border; within the limits of the pattern, lay out the border so that it creates a sense of continuity around the corner. With some patterns this could mean having a mirror image on each side of the corner. On others, you might try to create a continuous pattern that wraps around both walls. Some manufacturers offer square or rectangular medallions for corners; these eliminate the requirements of carefully matching a pattern or cutting a miter joint.

TOOLS & MATERIALS
▌ Wallpaper border ▌ Border adhesive
▌ Foam roller or brush for adhesive
▌ Wallpaper smoother ▌ Drywall knife
▌ Utility knife ▌ Steam roller
▌ Straightedge ▌ Sponge

1 Begin by cutting the border paper for all walls in the room, leaving each one a few inches longer than the actual wall length. For walls with outside corners, you will need to add an additional length equal to the width of the border paper itself to allow for the mitered corner. Place the first length of paper face-side down on the worktable, and use a foam roller or brush to spread the wallpaper adhesive on the back.

2 Loosely fold the paper into an accordion or concertina shape, with the pasted surfaces against one another. Take care not to crease the folds, because creases could cause visible lines in the paper after it is installed. Allow the paper to rest for about 5 minutes before installation—the moisture in the paste will cause it to expand, and you want this to happen before you trim it to fit the wall. *(continued on page 76)*

75

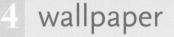

(continued from page 75)

3 If you begin at an inside corner, unfold 18–24 in. of the border and press it to the ceiling, allowing an overlap onto the end wall, with its back edge tight to the face of the long wall. The paste is slippery, and it will allow you to slide the paper to adjust its position. Move your hand along the strip, pressing it to the ceiling. Unfold the next section of the border, and continue with the application, working your way toward the opposite corner.

4 Use a plastic smoother or smoothing brush to gently work out any creases or bubbles, pressing the paper to the ceiling. Pay special attention to the edges of the border, making sure that the paper is bonded properly.

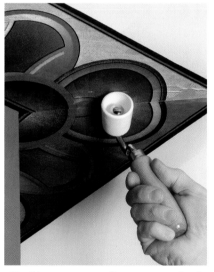

7 Align a straightedge with the wall corner on one end and the intersection of the outer edges of the border. Use a sharp utility knife to cut the miter joint, slicing simultaneously through both layers of paper. Use the same technique for a straight cut.

8 After cutting the miter joint, carefully lift away the waste from the top layer of border paper. Next, carefully peel back the remaining top layer at the corner to expose the waste underneath. Pull the waste away from the ceiling, and smooth the joint back together.

9 Use a seam roller to press both sides of the miter joint to the ceiling, ensuring a good bond. Apply only gentle pressure to the seam so that you do not force the paste out of the joint; this could result in a weak bond and cause the paper to peel away from the ceiling.

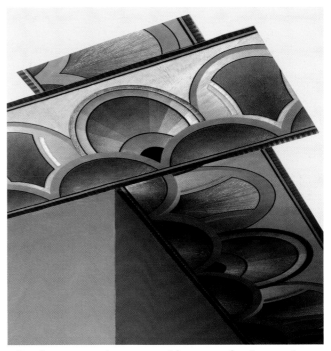

5 Trim the end of the border at an inside corner by holding a drywall knife at the junction of the wall and ceiling and running a utility knife against its edge. When you install the paper along the next wall, allow the border to completely overlap the first piece; then use a straightedge as a guide to cut the miter joint; remove the waste pieces; and smooth the joint as in steps 7 and 8.

6 If your room has an outside corner, begin your installation there to create a continuous border at this highly visible spot. In the photo, notice that the center of the semicircular pattern is aligned with the corner along both walls. Let the paper extend beyond the outer edge of the adjacent border so that you can trim the miter for a perfect fit.

10 Gently wipe the border and the adjacent ceiling with a damp sponge to remove excess adhesive. If left to dry on the surface, the paste can cause stains, ruining an otherwise perfect job.

11 Detail of matched outside corner joint. With this type of border design, it is appropriate to have the pattern appear as a mirror image at the miter joint—other designs might be better served by a different type of match at the corner joint. Because there are no rules that can be applied to all situations, use your judgment to determine the best treatment for corners.

80   INSTALLING A MEDALLION

82   CEILING DOMES

5 medallions & domes

Ceiling medallions provide a simple and relatively inexpensive way to dress up a ceiling. Although they are often used to surround a flush-mounted light fixture, hanging chandelier, or ceiling fan, they can also be used alone to provide a focal point for the room's ceiling. For a variation on the concept, you can also find molded rings of many different diameters, widths, and patterns that can be mounted on the ceiling; like a medallion, a ring can be used either on its own or to surround a fixture. By using a ring, you might completely eliminate the need to remove an existing fixture prior to the installation. Some medallions are simple, with unadorned flutes or beaded designs; others feature elaborate details that refer to traditional architectural motifs, such as acanthus leaves, floral patterns, or egg-and-dart carvings.

INSTALLING A MEDALLION

project

Although the traditional material for a ceiling medallion is plaster—and these are still available—most models these days are made of polyurethane. Because the installation is on the ceiling, you don't need to worry about the part standing up to physical abuse or wear and tear. And once the medallion is installed and painted, it's nearly impossible to identify the material.

Whether you choose a medallion of plaster or polyurethane, the basic installation procedure is similar. However, you will find that the reduced weight and slightly flexible quality of the urethane models make them easier to install.

If your decorating plan calls for a surface-mounted dome, the installation procedure is similar to that of a medallion without a light or fan.

TOOLS & MATERIALS
▌ Polyurethane medallion ▌ Screwdriver
▌ Marking pencil ▌ Stud finder ▌ Drill/driver
▌ Straightedge ▌ Caulk and drywall compound
▌ Construction adhesive ▌ Drywall screws

1 Many medallions are designed with a center hole to allow easy mounting around a light fixture or ceiling fan. However, if you wish to use one of these models without a fixture, you can purchase a rosette to cover the hole. Simply spread some construction adhesive on the back side of the rosette, about $1/2$ in. from the outer edge. Carefully position the rosette over the hole, and gently press to create a good bond. Allow the adhesive to set overnight before mounting the medallion.

4 Hold the medallion against the ceiling, placing the center opening over the electrical box. Use a soft pencil to trace around the outer edge of the medallion to mark its location on the ceiling.

5 Use a stud finder to locate the ceiling joists. Lightly indicate the center of each joist so it is visible on the outside edge of the traced circle. Hold the medallion in position; mark the joist locations on its edge.

6 Hold a straight edge across the face of the medallion, spanning between the marks on the rim, and mark the locations of screws for attachment to the joists. Drill and countersink pilot holes for the mounting screws.

2 For an installation around an existing fixture, you must first remove the light housing. Shut off power to the fixture by flipping off the circuit breaker at the panel box. Next, remove the glass lens or dome, and unscrew the lightbulbs from their sockets. Loosen the screws or nut that holds the fixture housing to the ceiling, and lower it to reveal the wire connections.

3 A typical light fixture will be connected to the house wiring with wire connectors. Support the wires that come from the light, and unscrew the connectors to expose the wire splices. In most cases the wires will be twisted together; carefully untwist the wires to release the light.

7 Spread construction adhesive on the back side of the medallion, keeping the outer bead about 1/2 in. from the edge to minimize squeeze-out. If necessary, you can remove excess adhesive using mineral spirits.

8 Reposition the medallion on the ceiling, aligning the previously marked pencil lines. Use long drywall screws to fasten it. Fill gaps with caulk. Fill screw holes with drywall joint compound. Sand the filler to blend with the medallion surface.

9 Completed medallion with light fixture installed.

CEILING DOMES

A ceiling dome can provide a dramatic and expanded sense of space in a room, but the very nature of this feature, requiring considerable vertical space, limits the possible situations where it can be used. In most cases, a dome is installed when a home or addition is first constructed, but it is possible to add one as part of a renovation, provided that the room is directly below an unfinished attic or other unused space. Unless you have considerable hands-on experience in building construction, you should leave this type of installation to a pro.

Because a dome extends into the space occupied by the ceiling framing and, depending on the specific configuration, can even extend well above the level of the ceiling joists, substantial modifications to the framing are necessary prior to installation. The manufacturer of a dome will normally provide detailed drawings of framing and support requirements. In addition to being fastened to ceiling joists around the rim, large domes often must be supported at several additional spots across their width by cables fastened to heavy framing members such as rafters.

Domes are offered in a vast range of sizes, shapes,

 ## WHEN THERE'S NO CEILING FIXTURE

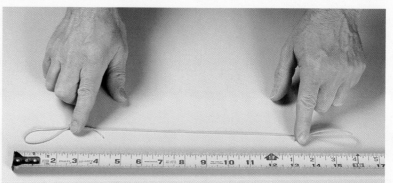

Measure the diameter of the medallion or dome, and divide that number in half to determine the radius. Tie small loops on the ends of a piece of string so that the total length equals the radius—keep in mind that, depending on the type of string, it may stretch slightly under tension, so you might reduce the dimension by 1/8 to 1/4 inch.

In cases where there is no light fixture or ceiling fan, you will need to determine the center point for a medallion or dome by measurement. Most often, these decorative items will be centered in the room. (But this isn't always the case—they could be placed in an alcove or near a bay window or fireplace, in which case you'll have to determine the center of that space). To center in a room, measure from the walls of the room to the center point of the ceiling, and place a light pencil mark on the ceiling. Drive a drywall screw partway into the ceiling at the mark, leaving the head of the screw about 1/4 inch below the ceiling surface.

Hook one end of the string around the screw head on the ceiling, and place a pencil through the loop on the opposite end. Hold the pencil perpendicular to the ceiling while you swing the string in a circle, marking the location of the outer edge of the medallion or dome.

heights, and styles—you can find round, oval, square, and rectangular models, with diameters as small as 3 feet and as large as 12 feet; some have very shallow elliptical arcs and others rise dramatically in semicircular curves. The most popular materials for domes are either fiberglass or polyurethane, and both provide smooth, paint-grade surfaces that will not crack if properly installed.

Before committing to a dome installation, be sure to check your local building code to learn of any specific regulations that could affect the job; it is the responsibility of the installer to conform to any pertinent requirements. It is also especially important that any modifications to the framing do not compromise the load-bearing properties of the ceiling joists. To that end, it is a good idea to consult with an architect or structural engineer when the job is in the planning stage.

In most cases, a dome should be installed directly to the ceiling framing—this means that the existing drywall must be removed from a substantial area of the ceiling at the beginning of the job. The framing modifications required for a dome installation will vary with the particular model you select. In general, it is necessary to create an opening in the ceiling by cutting out portions of some ceiling joists; to accomplish this, temporary braces must be first installed to support the joists that must be cut. In creating the rough opening, the ceiling joists that remain on the perimeter of the opening must be doubled to increase their load-bearing capacity and headers installed to carry the ends of those joists that need to be cut. Round or oval domes will also require the installation of angled joists to provide adequate backing for the mounting flange.

During the installation, adhesive is spread around the mounting

flange on the dome; then it is lifted into position and screwed to the ceiling joists. Large domes also have hanger clips on their top surface. Wires are connected to the clips and then fastened, at the opposite end, to rafters or other framing members above the dome to carry some of the weight; this requires access to the space above the ceiling. If a light is to be mounted in the dome, additional framing will be required to provide support for the fixture. After all structural considerations are addressed, new drywall can be installed and finished.

A ceiling dome and a marble column help to define this intimate eating area in this open floor plan.

86   MOLDING TYPES

86   INSTALLING CEILING MOLDING

88   INSTALLING POLYURETHANE MOLDING

91   CONSTRUCTING A CROSSCUTTING JIG

6 applied moldings

One of the most direct and accessible methods you can use to dress up a ceiling is to apply decorative moldings to the surface. By using the same techniques employed in creating wall frames, you can add an interesting dimensional quality to the room's ceiling. As a simple example, a molded frame might parallel the walls or surround a chandelier and be painted the same color as the ceiling. But you can also use this technique as an opportunity to bring additional colors to the ceiling, either on the molding itself or on the ceiling surfaces enclosed by the molding. You can apply a series of moldings that parallel each other or create an assembly that layers molded stock on flat lumber. You could also create molded frames and then fill them with wallcoverings or tin ceiling panels—the variations are almost without limit.

MOLDING TYPES

The largest selection of readily available moldings will be found in pine lumber. If you browse the racks of your home center or lumberyard, you will see both clear and paint-grade profiles, and you can install these items in any configuration you desire. Keep in mind that profiles that are intended for other uses are often appropriate for this type of use—these include panel moldings, casing, baseboard, and chair rail.

You will also find many molding profiles that are offered in MDF, or medium density fiberboard. MDF is made by mixing finely ground wood fiber with glue and forming it with heat and pressure into a uniformly dense stock. This material can then be cut and shaped with traditional woodworking equipment into moldings. In almost all cases, MDF moldings are sold with a factory-applied primer coating, eliminating the need for you to prime it prior to painting. For paint-grade work, MDF is an excellent choice, because its uniformly dense surface has no grain to telegraph through a finish, and it is generally less expensive than wood.

INSTALLING CEILING MOLDING

project

For a large frame molding installation, the only practical way to proceed is to apply one piece of molding at a time, and this photo sequence illustrates the technique. In this case, a chair rail profile is combined with a smaller panel molding to create a border around the ceiling. Small frames, up to approximately 36 inches per side, can be preassembled and then applied to the ceiling. (See "Assembling Ceiling Frames," page 88.) In most cases, you will find that painting the molding before installation is easier than waiting until you have mounted it to the ceiling. While the process of installation, both cutting and nailing, will probably cause some chips and nailholes, you can easily fill these and touch up the paint as required.

TOOLS & MATERIALS
▌ Molding ▌ Paint or stain
▌ Chalk-line box ▌ Stud finder
▌ Miter saw ▌ Construction adhesive
▌ Hammer or nail gun ▌ Finishing nails

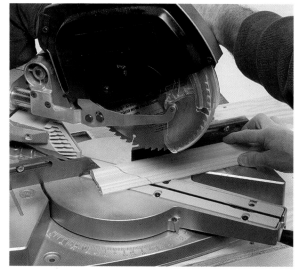

3 Use a miter saw to cut the corner joints for ceiling moldings. If your frames are either square or rectangular, the miter angle will be 45 deg.; for frames of different shapes, use an angle gauge to measure the total angle between adjacent sides of the frame and divide that number by 2 to arrive at the correct setting for the miter saw.

4 Begin the installation with a piece of molding that runs perpendicular to the ceiling joists. Hold the profile with its edge on the chalk line, and use finishing nails to fasten it to the joists. If there is no joist located near the end of the piece, you can use some construction adhesive to bond it to the ceiling surface.

1 Begin your project by laying out the positions of the molding on the ceiling surface. First, near each corner of the room, measure from the wall and place a light pencil mark to indicate the position of the edge of the molding. Then use a chalk line to connect these marks, leaving long straight lines on the ceiling.

2 In a rectangular or square room, you will find that the ceiling joists generally run perpendicular to two walls and parallel with the remaining two walls. Locate the points where the joists cross your layout lines. If you plan on repainting the ceiling, you can place light pencil marks directly on the surface to indicate the joist centers—otherwise, place a strip of low-tack masking tape on the ceiling and mark the joist centers on it.

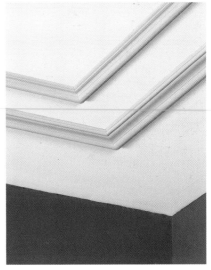

5 For those pieces of molding that lack solid framing above, use construction adhesive to bond it to the ceiling. Spread a bead of adhesive along the entire piece. Keep the adhesive away from the edges of the profile so that it does not squeeze out during installation.

6 Spread a bit of wood glue on the mating miter surfaces; then locate the piece on the ceiling, aligning its edge with the chalk line. Drive finishing nails at a sharp angle into the ceiling from both sides of the molding to hold it in place while the construction adhesive sets.

7 Finished wood ceiling molding.

project

INSTALLING POLYURETHANE MOLDING

nother option for ceiling ornament is to use moldings of polyurethane. These profiles are cast or extruded, rather than cut with knives, and this allows them to be formed into shapes much more complex than typically available in wood or MDF. In fact, polyurethane moldings can be used to replicate patterns that were traditionally executed only in plaster, but at a fraction of the cost; their

TOOLS & MATERIALS
▌ Polyurethane molding ▌ Spray paint
▌ Framing Square ▌ Construction adhesive
▌ Hammer or brad gun ▌ Finishing nails
▌ Nail Set

light weight and soft structure make them exceptionally easy to install. Many profiles are offered with companion corner pieces that are appealing for two reasons. First, the decorative corners can provide interesting focal points in the molding design, with elements that you could otherwise only provide with extremely expensive plaster or carved wood products. Second, by using these corners you eliminate the need to fashion mitered joints for the straight molding runs—they allow you to simply make square cuts on the molding and butt the resulting ends into the corner blocks.

You can cut urethane molding to size with normal woodworking tools, including a power miter saw, table saw, circular saw, or saber saw. However, if you only need to make square cuts on the pieces of straight molding, a simple shop-made jig will suffice. The most important factor in cutting the molding is the ability to reliably make a square cut. You can easily construct this jig with short lengths of lumber you may already have around the house. (See "Constructing a Crosscutting Jig," page 91.)

● ASSEMBLING CEILING FRAMES

If your decorating plan involves installing a series of small frames across the ceiling, your job will be much easier if you assemble the moldings into squares or rectangles and then mount them to the ceiling.

Once your frames are all assembled, carefully lay out their positions on the ceiling, marking the outlines with pencil marks or chalk lines. To install them, spread construction adhesive on the back side of the molding; press the frame to the ceiling; and nail to ceiling joists or use opposing angled nails to hold the parts to the drywall while the adhesive sets.

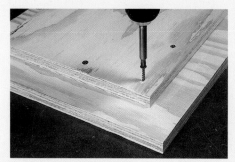

Construct an assembly jig for your frames by screwing together two sheets of plywood (with square corners). The base of the jig should be at least 2 x 2 feet for stability. The smaller top sheet should be set back from the edge of the bottom sheet by approximately 1½ inches to create a substantial ledge upon which the molding can rest.

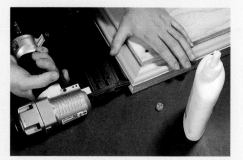

For each frame, cut the molding to length, with 45-deg. mitered ends, labeling them on the back side so you don't get confused in assembly. Begin assembly by applying glue to a pair of mitered ends, and then place the joint together in the jig, using the inner plywood panel as a guide to keep the corner square. Use a brad gun to drive fasteners through the outer edges of the joint to pin the parts together. Gently remove the part from the jig, and allow the glue to cure for at least ½ hour before working on it further. Assemble the opposite corner.

1 Decorative corners are available that are compatible with many different profiles—they have the added advantage of eliminating the need for miter joints at molding corners. For the best job, install the corners first; then fit the straight sections between them.

2 It's much easier to apply a finish to intricate moldings before they are installed on the ceiling, particularly if you use spray paint. Carefully follow the instructions provided with the paint to guarantee a quality finish. Here, a gold metallic paint is applied to the molding. Once installed, the appearance is similar to a gilt or gold-leaf finish. After the molding is in place, you will need to fill nailholes and touch up any small defects.

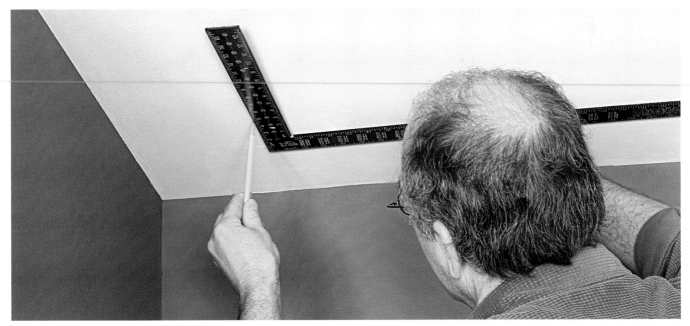

3 A framing square will help you in laying out the decorative corner pieces. First, measure the distance from the wall to the outside edges of the molding; then use the square as a guide to mark layout lines on the ceiling. Make light pencil marks so that they are easily covered with paint after you have installed the molding. *(continued on page 90)*

(continued from page 89)

4 Apply a small bead of construction adhesive to the top side of the corner molding, and press it to the ceiling, aligning the outer edge with the layout marks. Use a brad gun to drive brads into the ceiling at a sharp angle to hold the molding in place while the adhesive sets.

5 Measure the distance between the corner pieces; then cut the straight molding about 1/16 in. longer than that measurement to ensure a snug fit. Run a small bead of adhesive along the top side of the molding, and then "spring" the molding in place between the corners. Use brads to hold the molding in position while the adhesive sets.

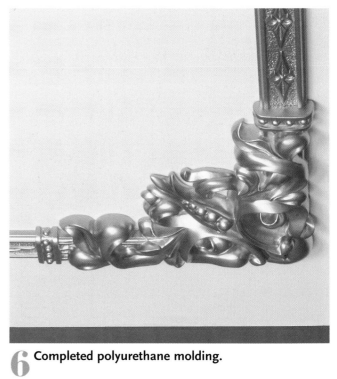

6 Completed polyurethane molding.

CONSTRUCTING A CROSSCUTTING JIG

It is not difficult to cut polyurethane moldings, as the material is quite soft and presents no serious challenges to the installer. If you have access to a table saw or sliding compound miter saw, you can certainly use either of these for the simple crosscuts required for this installation. However, it is not necessary to have one of these tools for this job— a simple handsaw is perfectly adequate. The most important requirement for trimming the molding is that you have the ability to make reliably square cuts, and a simple crosscutting jig is easy to construct. Here's how to make one.

1. Rip and crosscut ³⁄₄-in.-thick stock to size for your jig. You will need two pieces 3 x 24 in. and one piece 6 x 24 in. Clamp the narrow pieces to the edge of the wide board, and fasten them with screws.

2. Use a square to mark a cut line across the two sides of the jig; then extend the lines down the outside surface.

3. Carefully cut down along the layout lines until the saw teeth begin to scratch the bottom of the jig.

4. To cut the molding, place the stock in the jig, aligning the cut mark with the saw kerf on one of the jig sides. Keep the molding firmly pressed against the side of the jig while you make the cut.

94   SUSPENDED CEILINGS

96   INSTALLING A SUSPENDED CEILING

99   CEILING TILES

100 INSTALLING CEILING TILES

7 suspended ceilings and ceiling tiles

Installing a ceiling in a basement can be a challenge for a number of reasons. Access to the basement is often limited to a steep stairway, making it difficult to transport large materials like drywall to the room. Even if you were able to get the material to the basement, it may not be the best choice because using it would result in a sealed ceiling. Water piping, drainpipes, electrical wiring, and ductwork are usually located in the spaces between or immediately under the joists that support the first floor, and you must be able to get access to these utilities, something that would be difficult if the ceiling were sheathed in drywall or wood planking. A suspended ceiling is an excellent solution to this problem.

SUSPENDED CEILINGS

A suspended ceiling system is designed for the type of application described in the introduction to this chapter, allowing easy access to the space above the ceiling while providing a clean and attractive surface. These ceilings also offer considerable soundproofing benefits. By combining acoustically designed panels and physical isolation of the structure from the house framing, a suspended ceiling provides better soundproofing than other common ceiling designs. Suspened ceilings are quite simple to install; a typical basement ceiling can usually be completed in one or two weekends, and it requires only a modest collection of hand tools—hammer, drill/driver, tin snips, pliers, tape measure, level, utility knife, square, and pop-rivet gun.

Keep in mind that you can install a suspended ceiling in other areas of the home besides the basement. The system provides a quick and easy way to cover stained, cracked, or otherwise damaged ceilings. The logistics of the project may vary, depending on the existing conditions of the room, but the general installation procedure will be the same.

The Basics

The heart of a suspended ceiling system is a grid of interlocking metal tracks. First, you mount an L-shaped edge molding to the walls of the room and hang T-shaped main runners from wires attached to the exposed ceiling joists, spaced 4 feet on center. Then you snap crosspieces into the main runners at intervals of 2 feet. If the design calls for 2 x 2-foot panels, you can install additional crosspieces to yield the required-size openings.

Ceiling panels are sold in either 2 x 2-foot or 2 x 4-foot sizes. Most panels are made of a cellulose, mineral, or synthetic fiber mixed with gypsum, and are either $\frac{1}{2}$ inch or $\frac{5}{8}$ inch thick. A variety of decorative patterns and styles are available—some panels have square edges and sit on top of the supporting tracks, and other panels (called "tegular" edge) have a rabbeted edge that allows the panel surface to sit about $\frac{1}{4}$ inch below the tracks. You will also find some metal panels in the style of those used for a conventional tin ceiling. Metal panels are generally 2 x 2 feet and are designed to lay into a normal grid; however, because they are flexible, they require special clips to hold them flat against the supporting tracks.

In addition to normal opaque panels, suspended ceil-

Suspended ceiling systems offer a quick and attractive way to finish a family-room ceiling.

ing systems can accept translucent plastic or glass panels for fluorescent light fixtures or panels with an open-grid structure to provide ventilation or light diffusion. If light fixtures are to be a part of the installation, these need to be supported independent of the ceiling because neither the grid structure nor the panels are designed to carry additional weight. Consult an electrician for installation of ceiling light fixtures.

Manufacturers generally recommend that you set the height of the finished ceiling at least 3 inches below the lowest obstruction in the room—ceiling joists, ducts, or pipes. This clearance space allows you to tilt the panels into position or lift them out for future adjustments or access. Most modern homes have basements of adequate height to allow this type of installation, but in some cases, the clearance might yield a ceiling that is either too low for comfortable use of the space or in violation of local building codes. If in doubt, consult with your local building inspector before committing to a plan.

Ceiling panels are available in a variety of designs. The panels shown here provide a traditional finish, but some manufacturers offer embossed panels as well.

INSTALLING A SUSPENDED CEILING

project

If all rooms had dimensions that were multiples of 2 or 4 feet, laying out a ceiling grid wouldn't require much thought, but this is often not the case. In the real world, rooms come in a great variety of sizes, and you will need to adjust your layout to accommodate these dimensions. The first step in planning the layout is to determine the direction in which you will install the main runners, either parallel with or perpendicular to the direction of the joists. If you run them parallel, you will likely need to provide additional blocking from which to hang the runners.

In most rooms, panels that are adjacent to the walls (called border panels) must be cut to smaller sizes to accommodate room dimensions. The best practice is to lay out the grid so that the panels are of equal size on opposite walls, and this can usually be accomplished in two ways, determined by shifting the grid position to yield larger or smaller border panels. It's generally agreed that a ceiling looks better if the border panels are larger than one-half panel in size, so try to plan your layout accordingly. To determine the size of the border panels, first divide the room length by the panel dimension. Here's an example using 48-inch panels: if the room is 156 inches, divide that number by 48 inches to yield three with 12 inches left over. Add the 12 inches to 48 (the panel length) to yield 60 inches. Divide that total in half to yield the size of the border panels, 30 inches. You will then have two 30-inch border panels and two full 48-inch panels. If you are using 2x2 panels, use 24 instead of 48 as the operative number.

TOOLS & MATERIALS

- Level ▌ Chalk-line box ▌ Tin snips
- Suspended ceiling grid kit and panels
- Drywall screws ▌ Nails ▌ Pop rivets
- Pop-rivet gun ▌ Framing square
- Utility knife

1 Begin the ceiling installation by establishing a level line around the room at the height of the new ceiling. The finished surface of the ceiling should be a minimum of 3 in. below the lowest obstruction in the room—joists, pipes, or heating or air-conditioning ducts. Mark the height on a wall near the corner; then use a 4-ft. level to extend the line across the wall. Follow the same procedure on the two adjacent walls; then connect the lines on the last wall with a chalk line.

5 Snap the tabs on the crosspieces into the slots in the main runners. Normally, crosspieces are located at 2-ft. intervals. If your ceiling design calls for 2 x 2 panels, install short 2-ft. crosspieces between the 4-ft. ones, parallel with the main runners. When a crosspiece falls between the runner and the outside wall track, its free end should lie on top of the wall track. If desired, you can fasten these in place with pop rivets. (See "Fastening Runners to the Wall Track," page 98.)

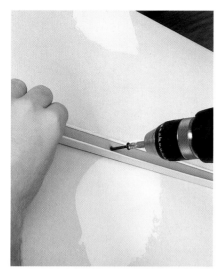

2 Cut the L-shaped perimeter wall tracks to length with tin snips. Attach them to the wall studs, with the bottom edge aligned on your layout lines, using screws or 6d common nails. Drywall screws will penetrate the tracks, but drill pilot holes if using nails. At inside corners, run the first piece tight to the end wall and butt the second piece against its leading edge. At outside corners, cut a 45-deg. angle on each piece to form a miter joint.

3 Lay out the position of the main runners on the ceiling joists and along the perimeter track; the main runners should be located on 4-ft. centers. Mark the location of the runner on the joists at either side of the room, and snap a chalk line to mark the intermediate joists. Drive nails or screws into the sides of every second joist, and hang a length of wire from each, twisting the top end around the fastener to secure the wire.

4 Check your layout plan to determine the location of the first crosspiece from an end wall. Cut the main runners so that a slot falls at that distance from its end. Hang the runners from the wires. Use a spirit level to check that the runners are level and straight from end to end, adjusting the wire attachment as necessary. When all is adjusted properly, twist the wires to secure them.

6 It is usual for the panels that fall along walls to require cutting. Measure the grid opening, and add about ³⁄₈ in. on each edge to rest on the supporting tracks. To cut a panel, use a framing square as a straightedge guide while you score the panel with a utility knife. Always use a sharp blade, cutting the panels from the face to avoid chipping out the finished surface. It isn't necessary to cut all of the way through the panel with a single stroke; make several passes with the knife.

7 To install the tiles, angle them through the grid openings and slide them into position. In the future, if you need to reach the space above the ceiling, you can simply slide one or more panels to the side to expose the area that needs work.

● FASTENING RUNNERS TO THE WALL TRACK

Suspended ceiling systems are generally well designed, taking most situations into account in the details of construction and in the instructions that many manufacturers provide. There is one area, however, that some manufacturers fail to address, and that is the intersection of the wall track with the main runners and crosspieces. Because the wall track has no means of directly engaging the other supporting members, they are left to float if you take no specific action, and they can be easily moved from side to side. Of course,

once the panels are installed, they keep the tracks from shifting, but if you need to remove the panels for some reason, the entire grid may become unstable. You can easily remedy this situation by using pop rivets to pin the crosspieces and runners to the wall track.

Pop rivets come in different diameters, materials, and lengths. For suspended ceiling work, you can select short rivets with a diameter of $\frac{1}{8}$ inch. Choose the finish that most closely matches the color of your ceiling track.

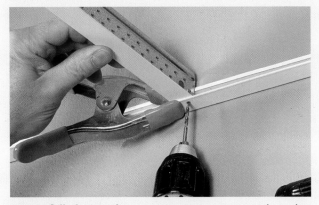

1. Carefully locate the runner or crosspiece end on the wall track so that the two members are perpendicular. Use a framing square to check that the parts are square; then use a spring clamp to temporarily lock them in position. Drill a pilot hole through both the track and crosspiece (or runner); the hole should be the same diameter as the pop rivet.

2. Install the rivet into the gun by first opening the handle and then sliding the end of the rivet into the gun opening. Push the rivet all of the way in until the flange rests against the nose of the gun.

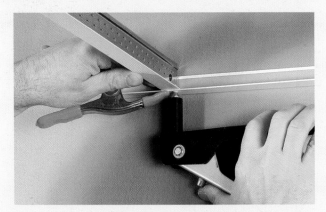

3. Push the end of the rivet through the holes in both the track and cross member; then squeeze the handles on the gun until the stem snaps off of the rivet, locking the parts together.

4. Finished pop-rivet joint.

CEILING TILES

While you might not consider the use of ceiling tiles in one of the dressier public rooms of your home, they present an economical and simple-to-install method of providing a new ceiling in a room with badly damaged or cracked drywall or plaster. Tiles were a common solution for ceiling renovation in the 1950s and 1960s, and they were so ubiquitous in family and recreation rooms that they became firmly associated in the popular culture with that time.

In those early years, asbestos was one of the components used to make tiles, but this hasn't been the case since the mid-1970s when laws were passed to outlaw the practice. Today, new designs and materials make this a reasonable choice for ceiling renovation.

Tiles are usually sold in 12-inch-square panels. Two edges on each tile have a small tongue and two edges have a groove, providing an interlocking joint between adjacent pieces. Ceiling tiles are soft and simple to cut—just use a sharp utility knife; a framing square is the perfect tool to use as a straightedge guide.

Ceiling tile designs have come a long way since those products of the 1950s and '60s. You can still find the traditional look, but many manufacturers now offer embossed designs on their tiles that resemble tin ceilings, wood planks, and elaborate plasterwork.

ABOVE Ceiling tiles are now used throughout the house. This kitchen benefits from the embossed design.

BELOW Tiles can be made to look like metal panels as shown here.

INSTALLING CEILING TILES

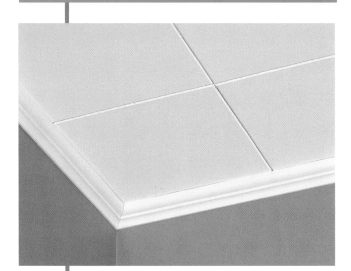

project

Depending on the size of your room, you may not be able to use only full tiles in the layout. When you must use partial tiles, plan the design so that there are equally sized tiles along opposite walls in the room. For example, if your room is 14 feet 9 inches long, take that extra nine inches and add 12 inches, yielding 21 inches; divide that number in half to yield the size of the border tiles at either end of the room—10½ inches. Before you actually start your installation, make a scale drawing of the room, and sketch in the actual tile layout that you will use. This will let you clearly visualize the ceiling and anticipate any areas that require special attention.

TOOLS & MATERIALS
▌ Furring strips
▌ Screws
▌ Ceiling tiles
▌ Chalk-line box
▌ Utility knife
▌ Stapler
▌ Staples ½ in. long
▌ Perimeter molding
▌ Miter saw
▌ Coping saw
▌ Hammer
▌ Finishing nails

1 Begin the installation by screwing 1x3 furring strips to the ceiling joists, 12 in. on center. The furring should run perpendicular to the direction of the joists. Locate the strips to accommodate the tile layout at the edges of the room. The first piece from the wall should fall with its centerline at the edge of the first tile.

4 Starting at one corner, align the grooved edge of the first tile with the chalk line. Provide a small space between the edge of the tile and the wall to allow for expansion. Drive two ½-in.-long staples through the flange on each edge into the furring strips. On the edges adjacent to the walls, you can drive 4d or 6d finishing nails directly through the face of the tile; drive the nails to within ⅛ in. of the surface, and finish with a nail set.

2 Measure the width of the first tile; add ¼ in.; and place a mark at that distance on the furring strips at both ends of the room. Snap a chalk line between those marks to establish a guideline for the outside edge of the first row of tiles.

3 Use a sharp utility knife to trim off the tongue from edges that will abut the walls. This will allow the decorative beveled edge of the tile to fit tight to the wall surface. If the wall is not absolutely straight, you may need to trim additional material off the tile edge to accommodate small bumps or bows in the surface.

5 A detail view of the tongue-and-groove joint on the edges of ceiling tiles is shown above. The wide flange at the top of the grooved edge is designed to accept staples to hold the tiles in place. Slide the tongue into the groove until the beveled edges are tight; then drive staples through the exposed flanges—there is no need to further fasten the tongue edge because it is held captive against the adjacent tile.

6 Select a molding to bridge the joint between the ceiling and wall surfaces. Here, a pine bed molding is installed; drive 6d finishing nails to fasten the molding to the top plate of the wall framing and to the furring strips beneath the tiles. Use coped joints at inside corners and miter joints at outside corners.

101

104 CORNICE ASSEMBLIES

106 CORNICE MATERIALS

108 CORNICE INSTALLATION TECHNIQUES

116 OAK CORNICE WITH DENTILS

122 PINE 6-PIECE COMPOUND CORNICE

126 CORNICE FOR INDIRECT
COVE LIGHTING

8 cornices

When you consider a room in an architectural context, every change of plane, as between a wall and the ceiling, presents an opportunity to bring new energy or focus to the space. The way you treat the surfaces can either accent or de-emphasize these changes. Different colors, textures, materials, and even more-subtle elements like sheen levels, all affect our perceptions; the careful and thoughtful use of these elements is the foundation of good interior design. In some cases, the transition from one plane to another calls out for some type of ornamentation or trim. And although there are some aesthetic disciplines that rely on crisp, unadorned corners, many architectural design traditions make use of applied moldings to provide these transitional embellishments.

CORNICE ASSEMBLIES

Cornice moldings have long been used as both defining and decorative elements, providing a transition between different surfaces. A cornice is defined as a molding, or an assembly of different moldings, applied at the junction of walls and ceiling. Many designs include what is commonly referred to as a "crown" molding, but this is not always the case. You can build a cornice from layers of flat lumber, or you can combine different molding profiles to form a large and elaborate assembly—many profiles that are used in cornices, such as base, chair rails, casings, or panel trim, are actually designed for other purposes.

■ **Cornice Styles.** Cornices of a particular type are often associated with a specific design genre such as Georgian, Victorian, or Arts and Crafts. The use of one of these characteristic motifs can strongly influence our sense of a room, carrying certain associations and expectations.

common molding profiles

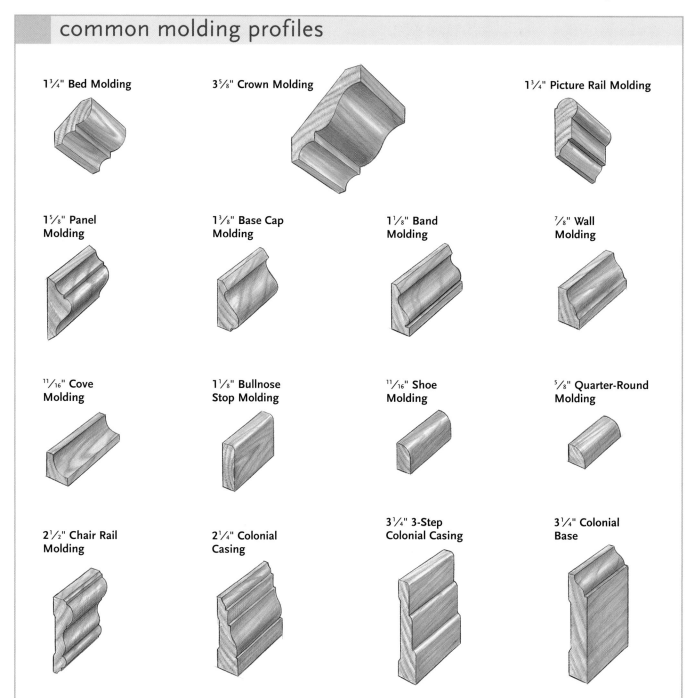

1¾" Bed Molding

3⅝" Crown Molding

1¾" Picture Rail Molding

1⅝" Panel Molding

1⅜" Base Cap Molding

1⅛" Band Molding

⅞" Wall Molding

11/16" Cove Molding

1⅛" Bullnose Stop Molding

11/16" Shoe Molding

⅝" Quarter-Round Molding

2½" Chair Rail Molding

2¼" Colonial Casing

3¼" 3-Step Colonial Casing

3¼" Colonial Base

While it's perfectly fine to venture outside of the formal and expected uses of any particular molding form, you should at least be aware of this issue, and consider it, before committing to a cornice design.

A cornice is frequently related in some way to the other architectural moldings in a room. Often a common profile is repeated in the base, casing, and cornice molding, perhaps in a slightly modified scale or with varying levels of complexity. If your room has a ceiling medallion, you could certainly link the cornice profile with the decorative elements that it displays. If the room is lacking in other decorative elements, you might use the cornice as the single eye-catching detail—in this case it can become the defining component of your design scheme. And if you are adding a planked ceiling, beams, or coffers to your room, a cornice molding can be an integral part of the design, serving as a bridge between the separate architectural features.

built-up molding profiles

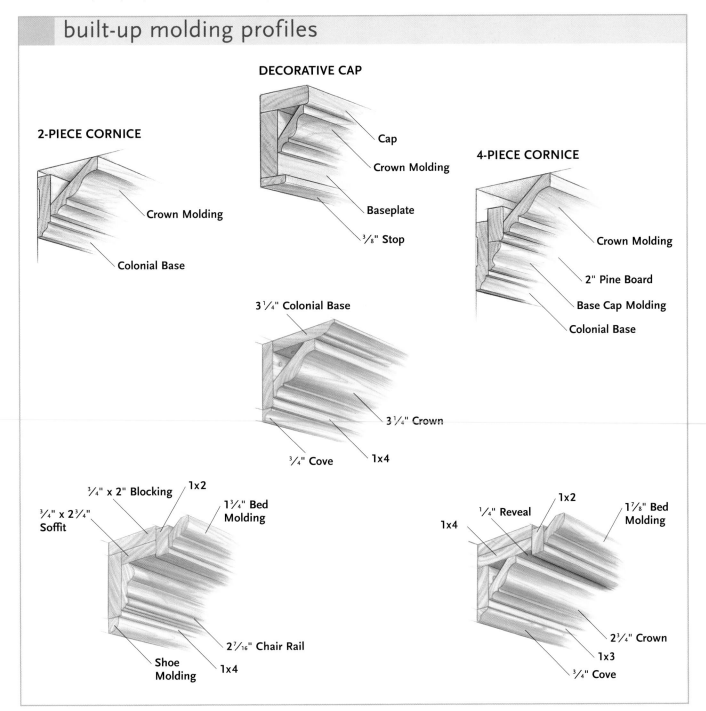

DECORATIVE CAP

Cap

Crown Molding

Baseplate

$^3/_8$" Stop

2-PIECE CORNICE

Crown Molding

Colonial Base

4-PIECE CORNICE

Crown Molding

2" Pine Board

Base Cap Molding

Colonial Base

$3^1/_4$" Colonial Base

$3^1/_4$" Crown

$^3/_4$" Cove

1x4

$^3/_4$" x 2" Blocking

1x2

$^3/_4$" x $2^3/_4$" Soffit

$1^1/_4$" Bed Molding

$2^7/_{16}$" Chair Rail

Shoe Molding

1x4

$^1/_4$" Reveal

1x2

1x4

$1^7/_8$" Bed Molding

$2^3/_4$" Crown

1x3

$^3/_4$" Cove

105

CORNICE MATERIALS

You can find ideas for cornice designs in many different places. Home centers and lumberyards usually offer an impressive selection of moldings, many specifically intended for cornice applications. If you cannot find a molding to suit your room, there are millwork houses that specialize in creating custom profiles. Many of these have extensive catalogs of moldings that they offer in addition to being able to create moldings from samples or drawings that you provide. (See Resources, page 180.) These trimwork catalogs generally have well-illustrated examples of cornice assemblies to further stimulate your design sensibilities.

In most peoples' minds, wood is the default material for cornice construction. And while wood is still the primary choice for trimwork, you do have other choices, each with its positive attributes. The most readily available species for wood moldings has long been pine, and this remains true. Pine profiles are sold as either clear or finger-jointed. Finger-jointed moldings are composed of

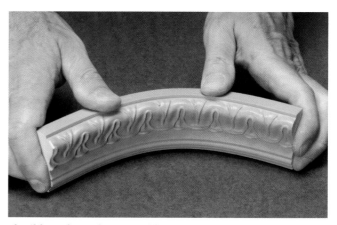

Flexible polyurethane moldings can be bent to follow most curved walls, allowing the easy installation of a cornice in unusually designed rooms.

short pieces of lumber, joined end to end, with small interlocking fingers that form a glue joint (hence the name). Finger-jointed moldings are considerably less expensive than clear stock, but because the individual pieces of lumber are not selected for matching grain, they must be painted, while clear material can receive a stained or transparent finish. You can also select moldings in one of many hardwood species; most are intended to receive a clear finish, with only poplar commonly used for paint-grade work. Each type of hardwood lumber has a unique grain structure and characteristic color. (Popular hardwoods are shown opposite, top.) Most also accept stain well, allowing you to further customize the look of the finished molding. You will find that hardwood moldings of red oak and poplar are commonly stocked in home centers and lumberyards, while other species usually need to be purchased from specialty millwork suppliers. When planning a wooden molding installation, keep in mind that pine and poplar moldings can easily be nailed by hand, but the majority of hardwood species require that you either use a nail gun or drill a pilot hole for each nail when hand nailing.

For paint-grade jobs, you also have the option of choosing moldings made of MDF, or medium-density fiberboard. This material is made of ground wood fiber and glue that is heated and formed under pressure into a uniform and stable composite. MDF can be molded like wood into any profile, and you can use normal woodworking tools to drill, cut, and shape it during installation. Most MDF moldings are sold with a factory-applied prime coating, which eliminates the need for you to prime it prior to painting. While moldings made

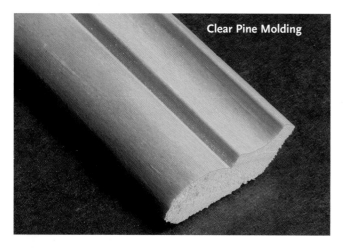

Clear Pine Molding

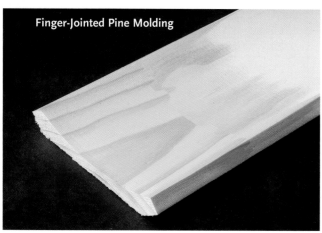

Finger-Jointed Pine Molding

of MDF are not the best choice for baseboard and casings that may be subject to physical abuse, cornice moldings are an excellent place to use this cost-effective material. Due to the hardness and density of MDF stock, installation requires either drilling pilot holes for hand nailing or using a pneumatic nail gun.

Another possible choice for paint-grade projects is the use of polyurethane moldings. This material can be extruded and cast in extremely detailed and elaborate patterns, allowing it to mimic classical plaster molding profiles that are difficult or impossible to execute in wood. It is extremely lightweight and very easy to install using screws and adhesive. In addition, most manufacturers of these moldings offer corner and joining blocks, so that you can design a project to completely eliminate the need for complicated miter, coped, and scarf joints—all a necessary part of a wood molding installation. Some companies also sell flexible moldings of polyurethane that can be used on curved walls; certain flat profiles can be bent to match the shape of a wall, while sprung profiles—those that sit at an angle between the wall and ceiling—must be custom-ordered to match the wall radius.

Once it is installed and finished with a fresh coat of paint, only the most discerning eye can spot a polyurethane cornice.

Mahogany

Red Oak

White Oak

Walnut

Poplar

Cherry

Maple

Birch

CORNICE INSTALLATION TECHNIQUES

If you are planning a D-I-Y cornice installation using wood or MDF stock, you will need to understand some basic concepts and master the skills associated with fashioning molding joints. While these are not particularly difficult to learn, you should not expect success with your first attempt; instead, purchase some inexpensive molding to use as practice stock, and repeat these techniques until you feel comfortable with their execution.

Outside Corner Joints

In most cases, moldings that meet at outside corners must be cut to form a miter joint, and for this you'll need a miter saw. A miter joint is one in which the material on each side of the joint is cut at an angle equal to one-half of the total angle measurement of the corner. For instance, on a typical 90-degree outside corner, each piece of molding is cut at an angle of 45 degrees. When flat moldings or plain lumber is mounted to the wall, this means making a bevel cut (through the thickness of the stock), and when those same moldings are mounted to the ceiling, they require a miter cut (across the width of the stock).

■ **Determine the True Angle.** To achieve a tight miter joint you must first determine the actual angle of the corner. It is not sufficient to assume that a corner is 90 degrees, because several factors can cause variations—poor framing technique, warped framing lumber, or a buildup of drywall compound are just a few examples. The most direct approach to determining the angle is to measure the corner using an adjustable angle gauge and then divide the total angle in half to determine the miter saw set-

CUTTING MOLDING FOR OUTSIDE CORNERS

There are two methods for cutting miter joints. For stock that will be mounted to the wall, use a bevel cut as shown in step 1. For stock mounted to the ceiling, use the method in step 2.

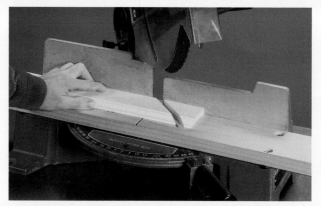

2. To make a miter cut on a flat molding, hold the molding flat on the saw table.

1. To make a bevel cut on a flat molding, hold the molding against the fence and rotate the saw to the desired bevel angle.

3. The most direct method of determining the angle of a corner is to use an angle gauge. Hold the legs of the gauge against the walls, and read the angle. The miter angle is one-half of the total measurement.

ting. As an alternative, you can cut a 45-degree miter on the ends of two scrap boards and hold them in place on the outside corner to see whether they fit tightly together. If the joint is open at the outside edge, the angle is greater than 90 degrees; if it's open along the wall, it is less than 90 degrees. Re-cut the angles on both pieces, and test the fit again, repeating the process until the joint is tight. Always keep in mind that both pieces must be cut at the same angle for a proper joint.

Scarf Joints

In most situations, it will be to your advantage to use a single length of molding to cover a wall, but there are situations where the available molding is just too short. At other times there are strategic reasons to use two pieces of molding, even when you have stock of adequate length to use only one piece; the most common reason for this

would be to avoid coped joints at both ends of a single piece.

When you find yourself in the position of needing to join two pieces of molding end to end, the proper technique is to fashion a scarf joint. In a scarf joint two pieces are cut with mating 45-degree angles, one open miter and one closed miter. This type of joint reduces the possibility of the joint opening up because of swelling or shrinkage due to seasonal variations in humidity. It also results in a joint that is naturally much less visible than a simple butt joint. When laying out a joint, make sure that it falls directly over a wall stud, and try to position it so that it is in a place that doesn't draw your attention when entering the room. In addition, if your cornice assembly comprises multiple layers of molding, stagger the joints in successive layers so that they fall in different places on the wall.

● SCARF JOINTS

In some cases, you may need to join two pieces of molding together end to end, such as when applying crown molding to a long wall. Rather than simply butting the edges together, use a scarf joint, where the two pieces are cut with mating 45-degree angles. You will accomplish two goals: the joint is less likely to open later; and when done correctly, the scarf joint is almost invisible when viewed from below.

2. Cut a closed miter on the second piece of molding, and then test the fit of the joint. When you are satisfied with the joint, apply glue to the mating surfaces, and nail the second piece to the wall.

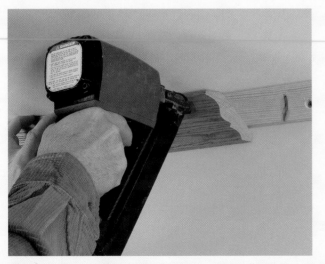

1. You can assemble a scarf joint on the wall. Cut an open miter on the first piece, and nail it to both the blocking and wall studs.

3. Use brads to pin the joint together.

cutting sprung moldings with a simple miter saw

Sprung moldings are those that sit at an angle between the wall and ceiling. The angle between the back of the molding and the wall is called the "spring angle." For most moldings, this angle is either 38 degrees or 45 degrees, but in practice, it's a good idea to check the actual angle with a gauge, particularly when using a sliding compound miter saw to cut the joints.

Using a Simple Miter Saw. An outside miter joint on a sprung molding requires a compound miter cut, a combination of a miter and bevel. If you are using a simple miter saw, the cut involves holding the molding at its appropriate spring angle. Position the molding upside down in the saw—the saw table represents the ceiling and the saw fence represents the wall.

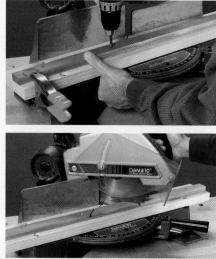

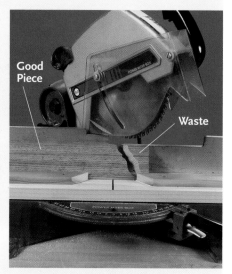

1 Create a positioning jig by cutting a straight strip as long as the miter saw table. Position the strip so that it supports the molding against the fence at the proper spring angle.

2 Screw the support strip to the saw table. Keep the screws outside the range of the saw blade (top). Make cuts at 45 deg. left and right to cut through the strip; remove the portion between the cuts (bottom).

3 This is a simple miter saw setup for a left-end outside miter (right-hand side of the joint).

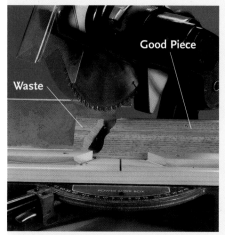

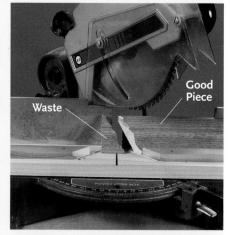

4 This is a simple miter saw setup for a right-end outside miter (left-hand side of the joint).

5 This is a simple miter saw setup for a left-end inside miter or coped joint (right-hand side of the joint).

6 This is a simple miter saw setup for a right-end inside miter or coped joint (left-hand side of the joint).

cutting sprung moldings with a sliding compound miter saw

When using a sliding compound miter saw to cut moldings, the stock is held flat on the saw table instead of at the spring angle. However, to achieve the proper cut, you need to set both the miter angle and the bevel angle; these can be adjusted independently on the saw. In fact, most saws have detents for the most common angles, simplifying the process. Be-cause the molding is held flat on the table, the angle settings are different from those used with a simple miter saw, and these settings are not intuitive; you must check a reference to find the correct settings. (See the table on pages 112–113.) Also, if the saw tilts to only one side, you will need to flip the molding around to obtain the proper angle combinations.

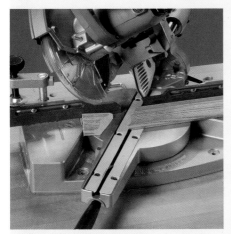

1 This is a sliding compound miter saw setup for a right-end outside miter (left-hand side of the joint). The bottom edge of the molding is held against the saw fence.

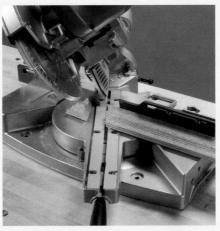

2 This is a sliding compound miter saw setup for a left-end outside miter (right-hand side of the joint). The top edge of the molding is held against the saw fence.

3 This is a sliding compound miter saw setup for a right-end inside miter or coped joint (left-hand side of the joint). The top edge of the molding is held against the saw fence.

4 This is a sliding compound miter saw setup for a left-end inside miter or coped joint (right-hand side of the joint). Hold the bottom of the molding against the saw fence.

Molding samples to illustrate the four basic miter cuts. It is a good idea to make samples like these and keep them for reference when adjusting the saw. It's easy to get confused as to the orientation of the molding, especially when using a sliding compound miter saw.

COMPOUND MITER SAW SETTINGS FOR CUTTING CROWN MOLDING

Corner Angle	52/38 Spring Angle		45/45 Spring Angle		Corner Angle	52/38 Spring Angle		45/45 Spring Angle	
	Miter Angle	Bevel Angle	Miter Angle	Bevel Angle		Miter Angle	Bevel Angle	Miter Angle	Bevel Angle
179°	0.31	0.39	0.35	0.35	134°	14.7	17.9	16.7	16
178°	0.62	0.79	0.71	0.71	133°	15	18.3	17.1	16.4
177°	0.92	1.18	1.06	1.06	132°	15.3	18.7	17.5	16.7
176°	1.23	1.58	1.06	1.06	131°	15.7	19.1	17.9	17.1
175°	1.54	1.97	1.41	1.41	130°	16	19.5	18.3	17.4
174°	1.85	2.36	2.12	2.12	129°	16.4	19.8	18.6	17.7
173°	2.15	2.75	2.48	2.47	128°	16.7	20.2	19	18.1
172°	2.5	3.2	2.8	2.8	127°	17.1	29.6	19.4	18.4
171°	2.8	3.5	3.2	3.2	126°	17.4	21	19.8	18.7
170°	3.1	3.9	3.5	3.5	125°	17.8	21.3	20.2	19.1
169°	3.4	4.3	3.9	3.9	124°	18.1	21.7	20.6	19.4
168°	3.7	4.7	4.3	4.2	123°	18.5	22.1	21	19.7
167°	4	5.1	4.6	4.6	122°	18.8	22.5	21.4	20.1
166°	4.3	5.6	5	4.9	121°	19.2	22.8	21.8	20.4
165°	4.6	5.9	5.3	5.3	120°	19.6	23.2	22.2	20.7
164°	5	6.3	5.7	5.7	119°	19.9	23.6	22.6	21
163°	5.3	6.7	6	6	118°	20.3	23.9	23	21.4
162°	5.8	7.1	6.4	6.4	117°	20.7	24.3	23.4	21.7
161°	5.9	7.5	6.6	6.7	116°	21	24.7	23.8	22
160°	6.2	7.9	7.1	7.1	115°	21.4	25.1	24.3	22.3
159°	6.5	8.3	7.5	7.4	114°	21.8	25.4	24.7	22.7
158°	6.8	8.7	7.8	7.8	113°	22.2	25.8	25.1	23
157°	7.1	9	8.2	8.1	112°	22.6	26.2	25.9	23.6
156°	7.5	9.4	8.6	8.5	111°	22.9	26.5	25.9	23.6
155°	7.8	9.8	8.9	8.8	110°	23.3	26.9	26.3	23.9
154°	8.1	10.2	9.3	9.2	109°	23.7	27.2	26.8	24.2
153°	8.4	10.6	9.6	9.5	108°	24.1	27.6	27.2	24.6
152°	8.7	11	10	9.9	107°	24.5	28	27.6	24.9
151°	9.1	11.4	10.4	10.2	106°	24.9	28.3	28.1	25.2
150°	9.4	11.8	10.7	10.6	105°	25.3	28.7	28.5	25.5
149°	9.7	12.2	11.1	10.9	104°	25.7	29	28.9	25.8
148°	10	12.5	11.5	11.2	103°	26.1	29.4	29.4	26.1
147°	10.3	12.9	11.8	11.6	102°	26.5	29.7	29.8	26.4
146°	10.7	13.3	12.2	11.9	101°	26.9	30.1	30.2	26.7
145°	11	12.7	12.6	12.3	100°	27.3	30.4	30.7	27
144°	11.3	14.1	12.9	12.6	99°	27.7	30.8	31.1	37.3
143°	11.6	14.5	13.3	12.9	98°	28.2	31.1	31.6	27.6
142°	12	14.9	13.7	13.3	97°	28.6	31.5	32	27.9
141°	12.3	15.3	14.1	13.7	96°	29	31.8	32.5	28.2
140°	12.6	15.6	14.4	14	95°	29.4	32.2	32.9	28.5
139°	13	16	14.8	14.3	94°	29.9	32.5	33.4	28.8
138°	13.3	16.4	15.2	14.7	93°	30.3	32.9	33.9	29.1
137°	13.6	16.8	15.4	15	92°	30.7	33.2	34.3	29.4
136°	14	17.2	15.9	15.4	91°	31.2	33.5	34.8	29.7
135°	14.3	17.6	16.3	15.7	90°	31.6	33.9	35.3	30

To set the miter angle, adjust the miter gauge on the saw. The bevel angle is set by adjusting the tilt of the saw blade.

Corner Angle	52/38 Spring Angle		45/45 Spring Angle		Corner Angle	52/38 Spring Angle		45/45 Spring Angle	
	Miter Angle	Bevel Angle	Miter Angle	Bevel Angle		Miter Angle	Bevel Angle	Miter Angle	Bevel Angle
89°	32.1	34.2	35.7	30.3	44°	56.7	46.9	60.3	41
88°	32.5	34.5	36.2	30.6	43°	57.4	47.2	60.9	41.1
87°	33	34.9	36.7	30.9	42°	58.1	47.4	61.5	41.3
86°	33.4	35.2	37.2	31.1	41°	58.7	47.6	62.1	41.5
85°	33.9	35.5	37.7	31.4	40°	59.4	47.8	62.8	41.6
84°	34.4	35.9	38.1	31.7	39°	60.1	48	63.4	41.8
83°	34.8	36.2	38.6	32	38°	60.8	48.2	64	42
82°	35.3	36.5	39.1	32.3	37°	61.5	48.4	64.7	42.1
81°	35.8	36.8	39.6	32.5	36°	62.2	48.5	65.3	42.3
80°	36.3	37.1	40.1	32.8	35°	62.9	48.7	66	42.4
79°	36.8	37.5	40.6	33.1	34°	63.6	48.9	66.6	42.5
78°	37.2	37.8	41.1	33.3	33°	64.3	49.1	67.3	42.7
77°	37.7	38.1	41.6	33.6	32°	65	49.2	67.9	42.8
76°	38.2	38.4	42.2	33.9	31°	65.8	49.4	68.6	43
75°	38.7	38.7	42.7	34.1	30°	66.5	49.6	69.2	43.1
74°	39.3	39	43.2	34.4	29°	67.2	49.7	69.9	43.2
73°	39.8	39.3	43.7	34.6	28°	68	49.9	70.6	43.3
72°	40.3	39.6	44.2	34.9	27°	68.7	50	71.2	43.4
71°	40.8	39.9	44.8	35.2	26°	69.4	50.2	71.9	43.5
70°	41.3	40.2	45.3	35.4	25°	70.2	50.3	72.6	43.7
69°	41.6	40.5	45.8	35.6	24°	71	50.4	73.3	43.8
68°	42.4	40.8	46.4	35.9	23°	71.7	50.6	73.9	43.9
67°	42.9	41.1	46.9	36.1	22°	72.5	50.7	74.6	44
66°	43.5	41.4	47.4	36.4	21°	73.2	50.8	75.3	44
65°	44	41.7	48	36.6	20°	74	50.9	76	44.1
64°	44.6	41.9	48.5	36.8	19°	74.8	51	76.7	44.2
63°	45.1	42.2	49.1	37.1	18°	75.6	51.1	77.4	44.3
62°	45.7	42.5	49.6	37.3	17°	76.4	51.2	78.1	44.4
61°	46.3	42.8	50.2	37.5	16°	77.1	51.3	78.8	44.4
60°	46.8	43	50.8	37.8	15°	77.9	51.4	79.5	44.5
59°	47.4	43.3	51.3	38	14°	78.7	51.5	80.1	44.6
58°	48	43.6	51.9	38.2	13°	79.5	51.5	80.8	44.6
57°	48.6	43.8	52.5	38.4	12°	80.3	51.6	81.5	44.7
56°	49.2	44.1	53.1	38.6	11°	81.1	51.7	82.9	44.8
55°	49.8	44.3	53.6	38.8	10°	81.9	51.7	82.9	44.8
54°	50.4	44.6	54.2	39.1	9°	82.7	51.8	83.6	44.8
53°	51	44.8	54.8	39.3	8°	83.5	51.8	84.4	44.9
52°	51.6	45.1	55.4	39.5	7°	84.3	51.9	85.1	44.9
51°	52.2	45.3	56	39.7	6°	85.1	51.9	85.8	44.9
50°	52.9	45.6	56.6	39.9	5°	85.9	51.9	86.5	44.9
49°	53.5	45.8	57.2	40	4°	86.8	52	87.2	45
48°	54.1	46	57.8	40.2	3°	87.6	52	87.9	45
47°	54.8	46.3	58.4	40.4	2°	88.4	52	88.6	45
46°	55.4	46.5	59	40.6	1°	89.2	52	89.3	45
45°	56.1	46.7	59.6	40.8	0°	90	52	90	45

Inside Corner Joints

To achieve professional results at inside corner joints on wood or MDF moldings, you will need to master the technique of cutting a coped joint, one in which one of the intersecting pieces is cut so that its end matches the face profile of the opposite corner piece. The alternative to a coped joint would be an inside miter joint, and although the miter is quicker to produce, it rarely results in a tight fit between the parts—especially because the process of nailing the molding in position tends to force the joint apart. Once again, this is a skill that requires practice to master, but once you learn the basics, the process will go quite quickly and the results will be worth the effort.

■ **Coped Joints.** In fashioning a coped joint, the first piece of molding is installed so that it butts squarely into the inside corner. Measure the adjacent wall, add a few inches for safety, and cut the next piece of molding with an open miter on the end to receive the coped joint—this is the same angle you would use if you were cutting an inside miter joint for the corner. The open miter cut will expose the molding profile that you need to follow. Use a coping saw to cut the end of the molding to the required profile.

■ **Using a Coping Saw.** When using a coping saw, most carpenters prefer to mount the blade so that it cuts on the "pull" stroke. This orientation allows you to better view the cut line and lessens the chance of binding or breaking the thin blade. Coping blades are set to create a wide kerf, allowing you to make adjustments in the position of the saw to follow the intricate shapes of many molding profiles. Hold the saw so that the angle of cut is sharper than 90 degrees; the cut should remove more stock from the back side of the molding than from the front—this technique is called "back-cutting" and it allows the coped profile to meet the adjacent piece along a sharp edge with no interference. Back-cutting also makes it easier to make adjustments to the joint, requiring you to remove much less stock to modify the profile.

Once the coped end is cut, check the fit of the joint against the already-installed piece of molding; the extra length of the molding will require you to hold the free end away from the wall while testing. Take care to hold the molding at the proper spring angle, because any deviation from its proper orientation will change the fit of the joint. Mark any areas that need fine tuning, and then use a rasp or file to make the necessary adjustments. Keep in mind that trial and error are a natural part of this process, and you shouldn't expect to have a perfect joint on the first attempt. When you are satisfied with the fit of the joint, cut the molding so that its overall length is $\frac{1}{16}$ to $\frac{1}{8}$ inch longer than the actual wall measurement. The extra length will allow you to spring it into position so that the coped end actually digs into the adjacent piece. This technique forms a tight joint and has the additional advantage of closing any tiny gaps that might remain.

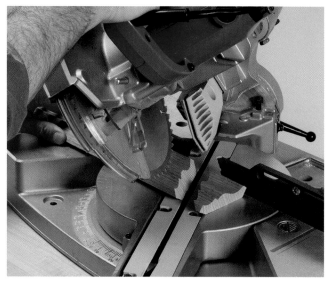

Prepare a piece of molding for a coped joint by cutting an open miter cut to expose the profile of the molding. The molding should be cut at the same angle that you would use for an inside miter joint in the same corner.

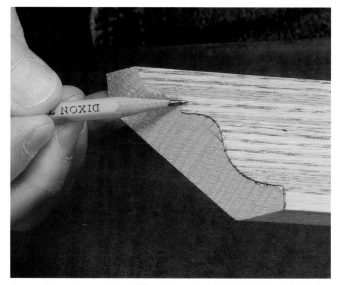

Sometimes it can be difficult to clearly see the cut line for a coped joint, so use the side of a pencil to outline the edge of the molding where it meets the open miter.

cutting a coped joint

1 Hold the coping saw at an angle greater than 90 deg. to start cutting the coped profile. Keep the saw blade about 1/32 in. to the waste side of the layout line.

2 Make relief cuts as necessary to keep the saw blade from binding in the cut (top). Continue the coped cut after removing some of the waste to free the saw blade (bottom). It is perfectly fine to cut from either edge of the molding; just remember to keep the blade angled to create a back-cut.

3 Use a rasp to further refine the shape of the coped joint.

4 It is often necessary to use a variety of abrasive tools to finish shaping a coped profile. Here a round Surform tool is used on the concave portion of the joint.

5 This is a finished coped profile.

6 This is the back side of a coped joint. Notice the clearance provided by the back-cut on the profiled edge. This will allow the adjacent molding to pass by the shaped end of the molding and will make it easy to adjust the profile for a tight fit.

OAK CORNICE WITH DENTILS

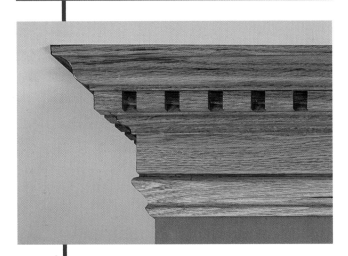

project

This red oak cornice uses a crown molding that is a stock item in most home centers. The crown is mounted on a frieze formed from a simple inverted baseboard, and the cornice is trimmed at its bottom edge with a traditional panel molding. The resulting assembly conveys the impression of a custom-made design while using readily available products—and without the premium custom price. Although this project uses red oak stock, you could use similar profiles in a paint-grade material such as pine, poplar, or MDF to reduce the cost or just to present a different appearance. Keep in mind that, for a paint-grade job, you can mix moldings of different materials, if necessary, and still get a first rate result.

While the labor involved in running three separate moldings is considerable, you will find that you become more efficient as you repeat these processes; the techniques for working each layer are essentially the same, only modified

to accommodate the particular nature of each trim profile.

The baseboard that is used for the frieze in this cornice is a 3¼-inch-wide flat molding with a ¼-inch radius on its exposed edge, ripped down to a width of 2⅜ inches. If you have trouble locating the same molding, you can always rip frieze material from plain ¾-inch-thick red oak lumber and round the edge with a router and roundover bit. You can also replace the panel molding with another profile to further customize the cornice design.

This particular design is well-suited to use in an Arts and Crafts-style interior, and would be most appropriate for a dining room, family room, living room, or library.

TOOLS & MATERIALS
- 2x4 lumber for blocking ▌Table saw
- Drill/driver ▌Stud finder
- Hammer, nail gun ▌Wood screws
- Crown molding with dentil detail
- Baseboard ▌Finishing nails
- Panel molding ▌Miter saw ▌Clamps

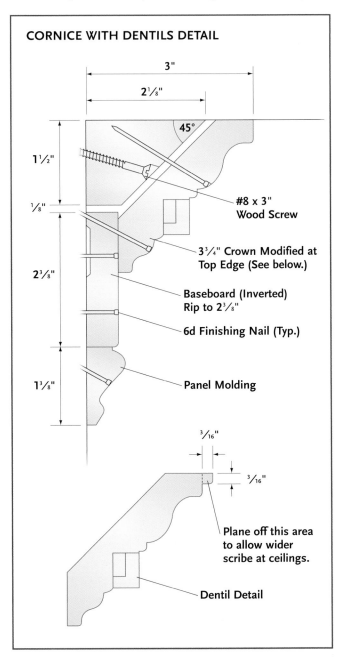

CORNICE WITH DENTILS DETAIL

3"

2⅛"

45°

1½"

⅛"

2⅜"

1⅜"

#8 x 3" Wood Screw

3¾" Crown Modified at Top Edge (See below.)

Baseboard (Inverted) Rip to 2⅜"

6d Finishing Nail (Typ.)

Panel Molding

³⁄₁₆"

³⁄₁₆"

Plane off this area to allow wider scribe at ceilings.

Dentil Detail

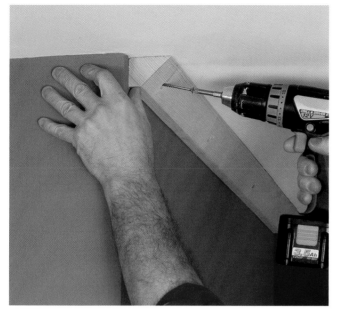

1 The spring angle for the crown molding is 45 deg., so rip 2x4 stock to that angle for blocking strips. Cut strips to length, and then drill and countersink pilot holes for screws. Remember that the strips do not need to extend exactly from corner to corner, because they are only there to provide nailing for the top edge of the molding. Use 3-in.-long drywall or deck screws to fasten the strips to the top plate of the wall.

2 At inside corners, leave space between the blocking strips to allow the first piece of crown molding to butt to the face of the frieze.

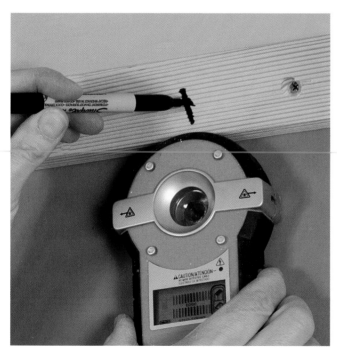

3 Use an electronic stud finder to locate wall studs. Place a mark to indicate the center of each stud on the face of the blocking strips for easy reference when nailing the frieze and panel molding.

4 Rip the baseboard molding to a width of $2\frac{3}{8}$ in. Whenever possible, use a fingerboard jig to keep the stock tight against the rip fence and to prevent kick back. Remember to always use a push stick toward the end of the cut. (The saw guard was removed for the clarity of the photo.) (continued on page 118)

(continued from page 117)

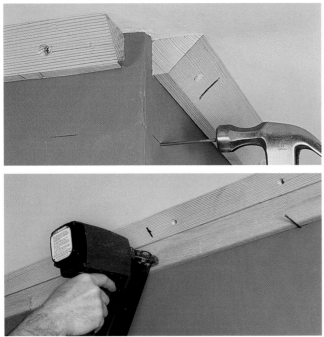

5 Place pencil marks along the wall to indicate the bottom edge of the frieze. Drive a finishing nail just below the mark at each end of the wall to act as a temporary support for the frieze while you mark its length and fit the joints (top). Use 6d finishing or 2-in. gun nails to fasten the frieze to the wall studs (bottom).

6 At an inside corner, butt the first piece of baseboard frieze to the adjacent wall surface (top). Cut a coped joint on the end of a piece of frieze stock, and then hold it in place to test the fit of the joint (bottom). Because corners are often not perfectly plumb, it is not unusual for a joint to be partially open on the first attempt.

using spiral anchors to install the frieze

In a perfect world, there should be a conveniently located stud wherever you need to fasten a piece of molding to the wall. Unfortunately, this is not that world, and there are times when you'll need a stud that can't be found. For a good alternative, install a spiral anchor in the drywall and use a screw to fasten the molding.

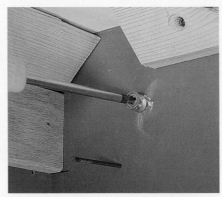

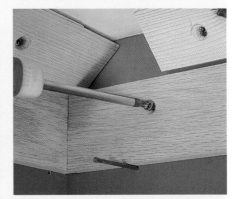

1 Support the frieze in position, and drill a small pilot hole (⅛-in. dia.) through the stock to mark the wall for the screw location. Position the hole so that the screw will be hidden by the next layer of molding whenever possible.

2 Remove the frieze from its support nails, and install a spiral anchor at the location of the pilot hole. Turn the anchor until the head sits flush with the drywall surface.

3 Countersink the pilot hole in the frieze, and then install the screw to fasten the molding in place. Use nails to fasten the rest of the piece to wall studs.

7 Make sure that you are satisfied with the fit of an outside corner joint; then apply glue to the mating surfaces of the miter; and nail the pieces to the wall. Use brads to pin the joint together.

8 Install the panel molding using the same techniques used for the frieze. However, if there are places where there are no studs for nailing, use construction adhesive between the molding and the wall to hold it in place.

9 When you cannot nail the panel molding to a wall stud, angle the nails to fasten the molding to the bottom edge of the frieze. In combination with some panel adhesive, this method should do a fine job of holding the molding.

10 Here is a detail of the installed inside corner joints of the baseboard frieze and panel molding.
(continued on page 120)

(continued from page 119)

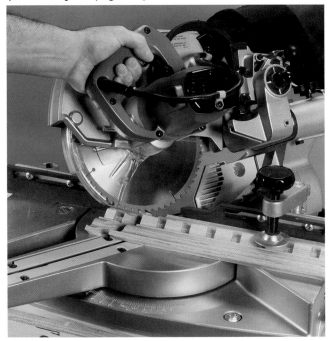

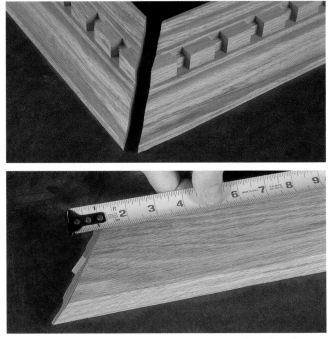

11 If you have outside corners as part of your room, begin the installation of the crown molding there as these are the most visible areas. Use the sliding compound miter saw to cut the outside miter joints on the dentil crown molding. Use your sample blocks as a guide in orienting the molding properly on the saw table.

12 Locate outside miter cuts to provide a dentil pattern that is balanced on opposite sides of the joint (top). Variations are less noticeable at inside corners. When measuring the length of crown with an outside miter joint, the length at the bottom edge must match the wall length (bottom).

15 Cut an open miter on the end of a length of crown molding stock to prepare for cutting a coped joint. To simplify the process, it is best to hold the molding at the spring angle. Use blocks and clamps to support the molding in the proper position (left). Hold a coped joint in place to check its fit (right).

16 Here is a detail of the completed inside corner joint.

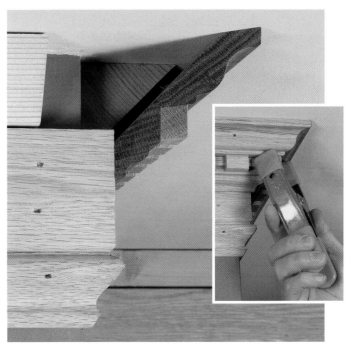

13 At an inside corner, install the first piece of crown molding so that it butts to the frieze on the adjacent wall. Nail the bottom edge of the molding into the frieze and the top edge into the blocking strip. If necessary, scribe the top edge of the molding to accommodate any irregularities in the ceiling.

14 Here is a detail of one-half of the outside miter joint on the crown molding. Note the space between the molding and blocking strip, which provides the ability to adjust the spring angle slightly. Do not nail the molding within 18 or 24 in. of the corner to allow adjustment. Apply glue, and use a spring clamp (inset).

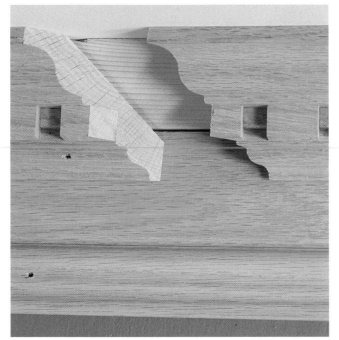

17 If you need to include scarf joints in your molding layout, plan the cuts so that the dentil pattern is not interrupted. For the least visible joint, locate the scarf cut so that it falls in the center of one of the dentils. Remember to apply glue to the mating surfaces of the joint before assembly.

18 Here is the finished oak three-piece molding with dentils.

PINE 6-PIECE COMPOUND CORNICE

project

A large room with a high ceiling demands a cornice with some size or complexity to feel appropriate, and this project has both. But even though the cornice presents an elaborate and elegant impression, the installation process is not particularly difficult. The final effect is the result of combining simple profiles, using basic molding installation techniques.

This compound cornice is constructed of six separate elements, with a rectangular soffit as its core. The materials are composed of mixed species, so this cornice is not suitable for a clear (varnished) finish.

Because this cornice has so many separate pieces, it is designed around a foundation box that can be built of either common pine or construction-grade plywood; from the box you can establish positive reference points for fabricating the corner joints. You can ensure that the corners are plumb and, at the same time, provide a dependable nailing base for subsequent layers of trim. And the foundation box simplifies the molding layout, as both the wall and ceiling frieze boards butt tightly to the box faces.

Begin the cornice by establishing chalk lines to indicate the outer edges of 2x2 blocking strips.

6-PIECE COMPOUND CORNICE DETAIL

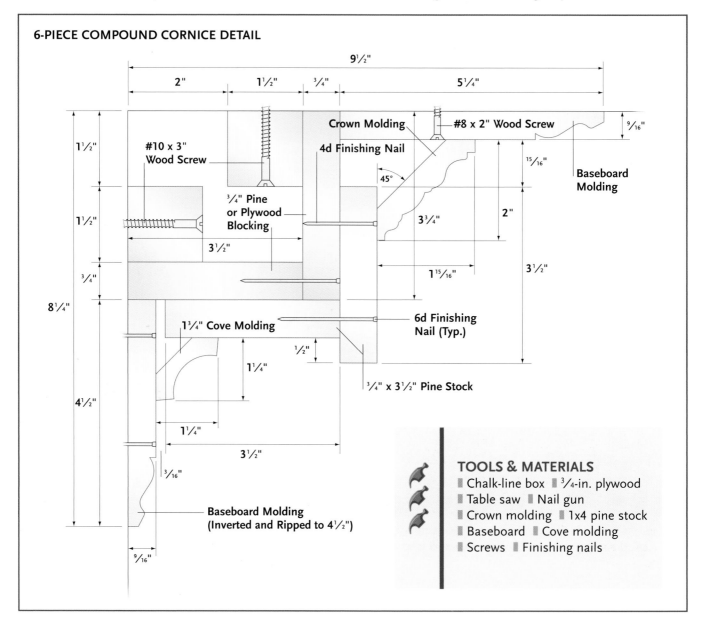

TOOLS & MATERIALS
- Chalk-line box ▌ ³⁄₄-in. plywood
- Table saw ▌ Nail gun
- Crown molding ▌ 1x4 pine stock
- Baseboard ▌ Cove molding
- Screws ▌ Finishing nails

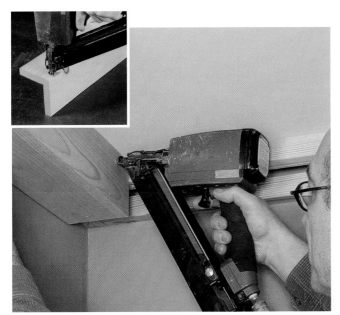

1 The foundation box can be constructed of either solid pine lumber or construction-grade plywood (inset). Rip pieces to width on the table saw—the box should butt against the ceiling blocking strips at both ends. Assemble the first L-shaped section by fastening the parts together with finishing nails or screws. Nail it to the blocking strips on the ceiling and wall. If there are any low spots or bulges, you will need to scribe the edges so that the box will be both square and plumb.

2 Build the next L-shaped section with staggered ends so that the bottom board can extend into the corner, behind the end of the adjacent box.

3 Here is a detail of foundation box at an outside corner. Note the staggered boards on the face and bottom of the box.

4 Cut the first soffit board to length, with open miters at inside corners. Hold the board so that its edge is flush with the face of the foundation box, using finishing nails to fasten it. Install the rest of the soffit boards. Note that there is a space of approximately ¾ in. between the back edge of the soffit and the wall. *(continued on page 124)*

(continued from page 123)

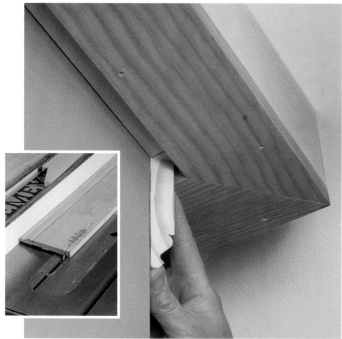

5 Select baseboard stock for the wall frieze. Use the table saw (inset) to rip the baseboard to a width of 4½ in. (Saw guard removed for clarity.) Cut appropriate joints on the ends of baseboard stock. The top edge of the frieze should butt against the bottom face of the foundation box—push the frieze into the space between the back of the soffit and the wall.

6 Install baseboard stock for the ceiling frieze. In those areas where there are no convenient joists, install hollow-wall anchors to the ceiling, and then drive screws. Make sure that you locate screws in the area of the frieze that will be covered by the embossed cornice molding. Cut miter joints for both inside and outside corner joints.

9 Cut bevel joints on fascia stock at outside corners. Apply glue to the mating surfaces of the joint; then nail the boards in place—remember to nail the joint together to help keep it tight.

10 Install the embossed cornice molding between the fascia and the ceiling frieze. As usual, cut coped joints at inside corners and miter joints at outside corners.

7 Because the baseboard frieze molding is quite wide, it can be challenging to have adjacent pieces align perfectly at an outside corner joint. To help keep the joint tight, apply a bit of glue to the mating surfaces of the joint and use brads to pin the outer edges of the miter together.

8 Install the fascia, allowing it to extend below the soffit by ½ in. Nail it to the face of the foundation box and to the edge of the soffit board. At inside corners, use simple butt joints between adjacent boards.

11 Finish the cornice by installing the cove molding between the wall frieze and soffit.

12 Here is the finished pine six-piece compound cornice.

CORNICE FOR INDIRECT COVE LIGHTING

project

Lighting plays an extremely important role in shaping how you experience an interior space. The possible types of lighting you can use have never been more varied; if you combine those choices with a range of placement and stylistic options, you have a powerful tool to modify the atmosphere in a room. One of the more compelling ways you can use light as a design element is to create a system of indirect lighting. Commonly referred to as "cove" lighting, this concept involves building a cornice or soffit to conceal the light fixtures that illuminate the ceiling area adjacent to the walls. In addition to providing a way to hide the lighting source, cove lighting offers an even and warm light that makes the ceiling of a room seem higher than it actually is. You can use this system as the main source of light or simply as an aesthetic accent. Cove lighting can bring attention and drama to a ceiling that also features another decorative treatment such as a border, medallion, applied molding, or dome. And by constructing a cornice to hide the light fixtures, you have the opportunity to add another strong architectural element to the room, compounding the appeal of this system.

For many years, fluorescent tubes were the standard choice for cove lighting, and they are still a viable choice. But for many people, the quality of the light from these fixtures is not appealing. Now, the availability of low-voltage xenon light fixtures has expanded the options. Offered in minitrack and strip systems, xenon offers many benefits: small size, design flexibility, lower operating temperatures than halogen bulbs, and dimmer options. As you might expect, the more elegant lighting alternatives demand a premium price, so it is important to consult with a lighting supplier before committing to a particular system. The size and height of the cornice can easily be modified to accommodate the specific type of lighting you select; most product catalogs offer guidelines for designing cove lighting systems.

The cornice featured in this project is a relatively simple design, constructed with readily available materials. The chair-rail molding used on the face of the cornice is available at home centers and is manufactured by House of Fara (www.houseoffara.com). The pine boards and cove molding can be found at any lumber or millwork supplier. Of course, feel free to personalize your cornice and replace the chair rail molding with another profile.

TOOLS & MATERIALS

- Chalk-line box
- 2x2 lumber
- Lighting kit
- Drill/driver
- 1x6 lumber
- Plate joiner
- Clamps
- Chair rail
- Cove molding
- Miter saw
- Nail gun or hammer
- Finishing nails

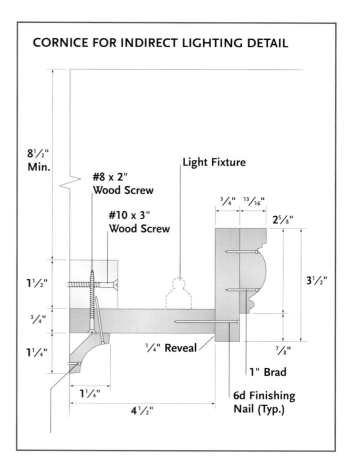

CORNICE FOR INDIRECT LIGHTING DETAIL

8½" Min.

#8 x 2" Wood Screw

#10 x 3" Wood Screw

Light Fixture

¾" ¹³/₁₆"

2⁵/₈"

1½"

3½"

¾"

¼" Reveal

⁷/₈"

1¼"

1" Brad

1¼"

4½"

6d Finishing Nail (Typ.)

1 The entire cornice structure is supported by strips of nominal 2x2 lumber screwed to the wall studs. Mark the height of the top edge of the strips on the walls near each corner. Use a chalk line to snap lines connecting these marks. Find the centerline of each stud, and screw the strips to the wall.

2 The electrical feed for your lights can be located in many different ways. If you find that the cable enters at the height of your blocking strip, mark the location and bore a ¾-in.-diameter hole to allow it to pass through. Of course, you should always make sure that power to the electrical cables is disconnected before you begin work.

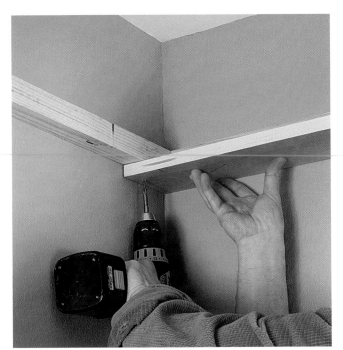

3 Rip the soffit boards from 1x6 lumber. Cut the first piece to length so that it butts tightly to the inside corners. Use a plate joiner to cut slots in the face of the board to form joints with the soffit on the adjacent walls. Screw the first board to the blocking, spacing the screws 6 to 8 in. apart.

4 At an outside corner, mark the soffit boards in place. Cut the boards to rough length, and temporarily screw the first board to the blocking strip. Hold the second board in place, and use it as a guide to scribe the length of the first board. *(continued on page 129)*

installing xenon light strips

Xenon lights are an excellent choice for cove lighting applications. Bulbs are available with an extremely long life, making them a good choice for areas that are hard to reach. Their lower operating temperatures compared with halogen bulbs, which tend to burn extremely hot, make them a safe choice, as well.

The strip system used for the project shown here is the Ambiance LX Lighting System from Sea Gull Lighting (www.SeaGullLighting.com). The basis of the system is a flexible cable that mounts in a plastic track. Individual lampholders snap onto the track at intervals as close as 2 inches. Lamps are available in a variety of intensities, and you can adjust the illumination to almost any situation. You can also install a dimmer to provide even greater control over the lighting. As a low-voltage system, a transformer is required, and a number of models are offered with different power ratings.

Always consult with an electrician or electrical supply house when planning your system to be sure that your design is safe, with adequate transformers for the number of lights you require—300 watts per run is the maximum recommended load for a 12V system.

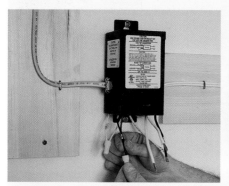

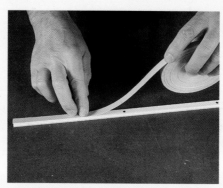

1 Install transformers vertically in an area with good air circulation. A normal 120V supply line is connected to one set of leads, and the low-voltage cable is connected to the second set of leads.

2 The plastic track comes in 4-ft. sections and can be easily cut. You can screw the track to the soffit with small screws, but it is much simpler to use a double-sided adhesive tape that comes in the kit. Press the tape onto the bottom of the track, and then remove the paper backer and adhere the track firmly to the soffit.

3 The low-voltage cable is extremely soft and flexible; simply press it into the track. You can easily bend the cable around corners. Track covers are available for use on non-illuminated sections of the cable; as an alternative, standard electrical conduit can be used to protect the cable.

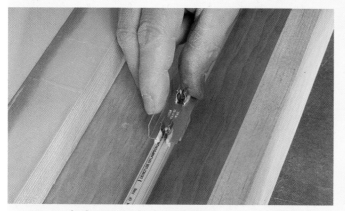

4 Push down on the lampholders to snap them onto the track. Each holder has small prongs on the bottom that puncture the cable to make the electrical connection.

5 The lampholders accept festoon lamps that easily snap into clips at both ends. Lamps are available in both 5- and 10-watt ratings.

(continued from page 127)

5 Temporarily screw the second board in place at the outside corner; then clamp a straight piece of scrap lumber flush to the outside edge of the adjacent soffit board. Use this as a guide to mark the length of the soffit. Remove it, and cut it to length.

6 Cut matching joining plate slots in the mating surfaces of the soffit boards at an outside corner. Screw the first board in place; then spread a light coating of glue in both slots and on the joining plate. Assemble the joint, and screw the second soffit board to the blocking strip.

7 To further strengthen the joints between adjacent soffit boards, toenail 4d finishing nails to fasten the outer edges of the boards together. Use a nail set to drive the nails flush with the edge of the board.

8 Simple butt joints are fine at the inside corners of the 1x4 fascia boards. However, to keep the joints tight, bore pilot holes for screws in the first piece of fascia at a corner. Position the first piece of fascia so that it drops $1/4$ in. below the soffit, and then nail it to the soffit edge. (continued on page 130)

(continued from page 129)

9 Install the second fascia board at an inside corner; then use a stubby screwdriver to drive the screws to fasten the corner joint. Because the pine boards are so soft, you do not need to drill pilot holes into the end grain.

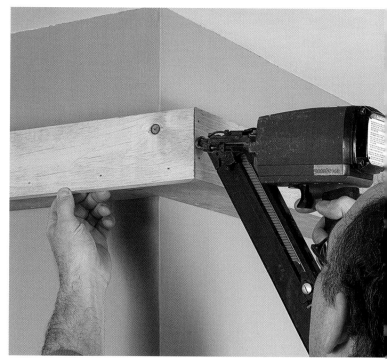

10 Cut outside bevel joints on fascia stock for any outside corners in the room. Apply glue to the joint surfaces, and then nail the joint together.

13 As with any other molding, it is best to mark the length of the cove profile at an outside corner by holding it in place and directly scribing along the wall.

14 Nail the cove molding to both the soffit boards and wall studs. You can use either 4d finishing nails or 1½-in. brads. Because the molding is quite small, it will easily conform to minor irregularities in the wall surface, covering any gaps between the soffit and the wall.

11 Begin installing the chair-rail molding by cutting square ends on the stock to butt against the fascia at an inside corner. Use 1-in.-long brads to fasten the molding to the fascia.

12 Cut coped joints in chair-rail stock at inside corners and bevel joints at outside corners. Because the molding is a flat profile and the material is soft, cutting the joints is not difficult.

15 Here is the finished cornice with indirect lighting.

134 TYPES OF PLANK CEILINGS

136 INSTALLING A PLANK CEILING

9 plank ceilings

You don't have to be a professional carpenter to tackle a plank ceiling project. Using only basic woodworking techniques, you can achieve impressive results—and the wide selection of available materials and finishes will allow you to tailor the ultimate look of your ceiling to fit your own particular decorating plan. Whether you select boards of hardwood or softwood, the installation technique is basically the same.

Plank ceilings can be installed in almost any type of room or location, from basements to finished attics. This type of treatment is especially effective in rooms that have cathedral ceilings—one attractive and popular approach combines plank ceiling with applied beams to suggest "post and beam" construction—but can also be done on a flat ceiling.

TYPES OF PLANK CEILINGS

The materials that are suitable for ceiling applications range from plain, square-edge boards to prefinished kits specifically designed for ceilings. Depending on the look you wish to achieve, materials as coarse as recycled barn siding and as refined as highly polished walnut are all valid options. As a starting point, the most readily available and popular choices for ceilings are to be found in the softwood species. Pine boards come in nominal one-by stock with edges milled to tongue-and-groove or ship-lap joints; these boards are most often 1x6 material (actual dimensions $3/4$ x $5^1/2$ inch), with any of a variety of patterns milled into the board faces, including chamfers, V-grooves, beads, and flutes. In most cases you will find that the lumber is offered in a "knotty" grade, but select or clear grades are usually available, although they may require a special order. Another popular material is commonly known as "beaded fir ceiling stock" and is traditionally used for porch ceilings and wainscoting. Milled from Douglas fir lumber and often quarter-sawn to yield straight, even grain patterns, this is an excellent choice for rooms where you want a warm, casual look. You will find this material in a variety of sizes, varying with location and supplier. It is generally somewhat thinner than normal one-by stock, ranging from $3/8$ to $5/8$ inch thick and $3^1/2$ or 4 inches wide.

Most home centers carry some bundled kits that can be used for either wainscoting or ceiling planks; these are offered in a variety of wood species. These planks are usually very thin, measuring $1/4$ inch or $5/16$ inch with tongue-and-groove edges. Although the material can seem overly flexible and flimsy when you first examine it, once it is installed, with interlocking joints, it forms a perfectly acceptable ceiling surface.

Ceiling Plank Kits. Some manufacturers of suspended ceiling materials also offer ceiling plank systems; these are formed of medium-density fiberboard with an applied vinyl, plastic laminate, or paint surface, requiring no additional finishing. Most of these systems use a proprietary installation method, employing clips to hold the planks to the ceiling. If you are considering one of these systems, be sure that you read and understand the manufacturer's installation instructions before purchasing the product, and if you decide to use the material, carefully follow the directions.

Finished Looks. Ceiling planking can be installed by itself or in conjunction with a crown molding. Of course, the decision to use a molding will depend on the specifics of your overall room design. But when appropriate, adding a molding to the job provides two distinct benefits. First, the molding covers the junction between the ceiling and walls, making your installation much simpler because you don't need to spend time forming tight joints at those points. Second, the crown provides an opportunity for an additional decorative element that creates a graceful transition between the wall and ceiling surfaces.

OPPOSITE Beaded fir ceiling stock is often used on porch ceilings, but it is a good choice for interior rooms where a casual look is desired. Pine 1x6 is often sold with one smooth face and one face that features a beaded profile.

ABOVE Manufacturers' kits usually include some sort of proprietary installation method.

RIGHT The planks in this ceiling add to the cottage charm of this country kitchen.

INSTALLING A PLANK CEILING

project

In the early stages of planning your project, measure the dimensions of the room and calculate the total area of the ceiling; then add 15 or 20 percent to that number (for waste) to arrive at the material you will need for the job. If you plan to install perimeter moldings as part of the job, add up the length of all walls in the room, but in this case 10 or 15 percent additional for waste should be sufficient.

Although different types of planking will require adjustments in specific technique, there are some general installation principles that should apply. The photo illustrations demonstrate the installation of 1x6 tongue-and-groove pine boards, but you can use them as a guide for most varieties of wood planking.

While you can certainly wait until the ceiling is complete to apply a finish, you will find it much easier and less messy to apply the finish before you install the boards. Begin by lightly sanding the exposed surfaces to remove any scratches, dirt, and mill marks.

TOOLS & MATERIALS
▎ Tongue-and-groove planking
▎ Stain or paint ▎ Stud finder
▎ Chalk-line box ▎ Miter saw
▎ Nail gun ▎ Furring strips
▎ Drill/driver ▎ Molding (if necessary)

1 Carefully remove any sanding dust from the boards; then apply the first coat of stain, paint, or clear finish as desired. Follow the instructions on the particular finishing material for subsequent coats. Keep in mind that the installation will inevitably result in some nicks and nailholes that will require attention, but it is much simpler to make these small "touch-up" repairs than to do the entire job upside down.

4 Most of the nailing to secure the planks is done by angling the nail just below the tongue so that it will be largely hidden by the subsequent board. This technique is called "blind" nailing and will leave very few nailholes to fill. The angled nails have the additional advantage of driving the boards together to create tighter joints.

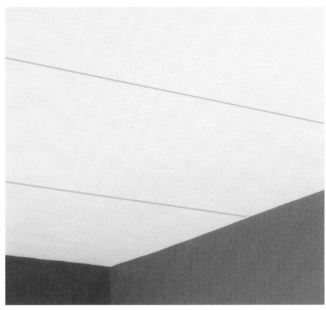

2 Use a stud finder to locate all of the ceiling joists in the room. Mark the center of each joist near its intersection with the walls; then snap a chalk line to connect these marks. This provides you with a map of the joists for direct nailing of planks or installation of furring strips.

3 If you wish to install the planks perpendicular to the direction of the ceiling joists, you can directly nail them through the ceiling surface. For an installation that will include perimeter molding, simply butt the grooved edge of the first board against the wall surface. If no molding will be used, rip the chamfered and grooved edge off the board to provide a square joint. Nail directly through the face of the board.

5 To install boards parallel with the direction of the ceiling joists, you will need to first mount furring strips perpendicular to the joists. Begin by establishing the spacing of the strips, 16 in. on center; then mark chalk lines to indicate the edge of each strip. Cut the strips to length so that they butt lightly against the walls, and screw them to the ceiling joist using drywall screws. End joints should fall at the center of a ceiling joist.

6 A sliding miter saw is a great tool to trim ceiling boards to size with perfectly square end cuts. However, for those without access to this tool, you can use a table saw, radial-arm saw, circular saw, saber saw, or ordinary handsaw and still get great results.
(continued on page 138)

(continued from page 137)

7 Whenever a board is not long enough to extend from wall to wall, you will need to form a butt joint. Make sure that these joints always fall directly over the centerline of a ceiling joist or furring strip so that you can firmly fasten the ends of both boards to the framing support.

8 It's not unusual to encounter some difficulty in fitting tongue-and-groove boards together. Small irregularities in the surface of the board, a warped edge, or a swelled or damaged tongue can cause resistance in the joint. One way to coax the parts together without causing damage is to use a short cutoff of the stock as a nailing block. Fit the grooved edge of the block over the tongue of the offending board and tap with a hammer.

11 Place strips of masking tape along the walls; then mark the location of stud centers on the tape. Cut the first piece of crown molding to length; then hold it in position with its square ends butting tightly to the end walls. Nail the molding to the ceiling boards and to each wall stud.

12 Cut a coped joint on the end of the second piece of crown molding, and test its fit against the first piece of installed molding. Use a rasp, knife, or sandpaper to adjust the joint until it fits tightly; then nail it in place.

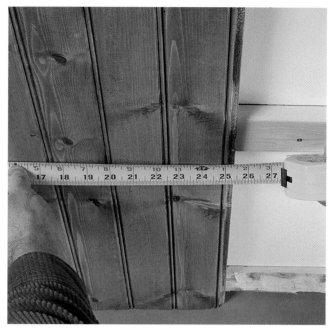

9 If your room has ceiling light fixtures, you will need to cut the planking to accommodate the openings. Measure the distance from the edge of the last board before the electrical box to the edge of the box. Use a box to trace the shape on the next board; then use a saber saw to make the cutout. Because you are adding material of substantial thickness to the ceiling, you may need to install a box extension to remount the fixture.

10 It is easy to have the boards start to wander from a perfectly parallel alignment. Check this situation by measuring from the starting wall to the edge of the tongue at three or four points across the room, every third row of planks. If you find a discrepancy, make a corrective adjustment in the next course. Rip the last board to width, cutting waste stock off the tongue edge, and slide it into position.

13 Finished plank ceiling.

Exposed ceiling boards offer another option. Paint the boards and rafters the same or use a contrasting color.

142 TYPES OF PANELS

143 WORKING WITH SHEET METAL

145 INSTALLING A TIN CEILING

10 tin ceilings

If you've ever admired a beautiful tin ceiling in a historic building, you might be surprised to know that the same material is available for use in your own home. And even more surprising is the fact that this is a material that you can install yourself using only a modest collection of hand tools.

Despite their generic name, tin ceiling panels are offered in several different materials, none of them solid tin. The most common material for these panels is sheet steel. You will also find panels in both solid copper and brass, and others with a chrome surface. Unfinished panels allow you to customize the look of your ceiling. You will also find a selection of cornice moldings. These provide a way to finish the edges of the ceiling, creating an elegant transition between the horizontal and vertical surfaces.

TYPES OF PANELS

Ceiling panels are offered in many different embossed patterns—some designs have strong links to a particular design scheme such as Art Deco or Victorian, but many are appropriate for a wide range of decorative styles. A typical panel features a pattern that repeats at a regular interval over the entire surface; intervals of 3, 4, 6, and 12 inches are the most common. The variety of pattern sizes allows you to select a design with a scale that best suits the size of your room. As a general rule, panels with smaller patterns are better suited to small rooms.

Tin ceilings are traditionally installed by nailing them in place, and panels for that type of installation are available in 24 x 24-, 24 x 48- and 24 x 96-inch sizes. For those that wish to install a suspended ceiling system, there are also panels made specifically for that use that are either 24 x 24 or 24 x 48 inches; some of these have a recessed lip that allows the face of the panel to sit lower than the supporting tracks. Some manufacturers also offer snap-on covers for the supporting tracks that match the ceiling panels.

■ **Ceiling Layout.** The layout of your ceiling will depend largely on the particular pattern you choose. Panels can be cut to a smaller size, but for the job to have a professional look, you should only make cuts between the repeating elements of the pattern, not through them. In practice, this means that it is very possible that the main ceiling panels will not cover the entire ceiling, wall to wall, especially when using a larger panel design. This can be compounded by the use of a cornice molding that also extends toward the center of the room; you don't want to create a condition where the molding covers part of the panel design. Fortunately, there is a ready solution for this situation. Filler panels are available that are intended for use as a border between the wall or cornice molding and the central patterned ceiling. These have a uniformly textured surface that can be cut to any size without consideration of a pattern. To use these filler panels, you must design your ceiling so that the main patterned area is centered in the room, with space for the filler border on all edges. Because filler panels are typically 24 inches wide, you should consider that dimension to be the maximum width of your border. Given that room dimensions can vary, it may not be possible to have the same width border on all walls, but you should always design the ceiling so that the borders along opposite walls are equal.

At the edges of the room, where the ceiling meets the walls, a metal cornice molding can be nailed right over the filler panel material. Cornice moldings are available in a range of styles and sizes to complement the designs of the ceiling panels. If you wish, it is also possible to install wood cornice trim instead of metal. In that case, you can use a single molding, or a combination of moldings to fashion your own cornice design. For the best result, the cornice should be installed after the ceiling is complete.

Tin ceilings aren't really solid tin; they come in a variety of materials, including copper.

Cornice moldings for tin ceilings provide a graceful transition between the ceiling and wall.

WORKING WITH SHEET METAL

Working with tin ceiling panels is not at all like working with wood—you need to have a very different expectation of how the material will behave and what is possible. In particular, joints that you form in sheet metal will not be nearly as precise as those in wood; this is due to two factors. First, the metal panels are extremely flexible and can distort quite easily as you handle them; as a result, even an accurately cut joint may not align exactly as expected. And second, cuts made to sheet metal are rarely perfect— some wavering from the intended layout line is inevitable. To further complicate matters, overlapping seams may not align perfectly, resulting in gaps between the layers.

Fortunately, there are simple methods of handling these situations. Because open seams and joints are frequent occurrences in tin ceiling work, a technique called "caulking" is used to seal seams and adjust the fit of joints. (See step 20, page 149.) To do this, use a hammer to gently tap the pointed end of a common 16d nail, holding the nailhead against the metal to close the open joint; you can also use a small wood block or dowel instead of a nail.

Even after "caulking" open seams and joints, it is usual to have some remaining gaps, especially at the junction of cornice moldings and both wall and ceiling surfaces. This is where the other type of caulking comes in—the kind that comes in a tube. If your ceiling is to be painted or has a factory-applied colored finish, you can use a matching latex caulk to fill spaces. For ceilings with an unpainted steel, copper, or brass finish, you should use clear silicone caulk as a gap filler.

143

Prepare the Ceiling

In order to install a traditional tin ceiling, you need to do some preparatory work. Ceiling panels are typically nailed in place, but to do so you need to provide a substrate that will accept and hold the nails. There are two generally accepted ways to do this, and predictably, each has its pros and cons. In the first method, illustrated in the project photos on the following pages, you will cover the entire ceiling with ½-inch-thick construction-grade plywood, screwing the sheets to the ceiling joists. This method is the more expensive of the two, and it is awkward to support the sheets until they are initially fastened. However, it has the advantage of guaranteeing that you can drive nails anywhere they might be required.

For the second system, you would screw furring strips perpendicular to the ceiling joists, 12 inches on center, to provide solid fastening along the panel seams. This layout must accurately reflect the ceiling design, so considerable care is required in planning the strip placement. It is also necessary to provide crosspieces at the ends of each panel. This system is easier to accomplish if you must work alone, and the cost of furring is less than the cost of plywood, but it also has some drawbacks. First, you must precisely locate the strips to fall along the panel seams; furring is also required at the ceiling edge for the cornice molding. Next, individual strips are likely to follow small dips or humps in the ceiling, so you may need to place shims between the furring and ceiling to provide a level mounting surface. It is also awkward, and somewhat difficult, to fasten cross blocks to support the panel ends, because they must be toenailed into the thin edges of the long furring strips rather than screwed to the joists.

● INSTALLING FURRING STRIPS FOR A TIN CEILING

If you decide to use furring strips for your tin ceiling, begin by carefully laying out the locations of the strips to correspond with panel seams. The furring must run perpendicular to the direction of the ceiling joists, and the panel joints should fall along the centerline of each strip. Carefully follow your layout plan; place marks on the ceiling along opposite walls; and snap a chalk line to indicate the edge of each strip.

1. Screw furring strips to the ceiling joists with long drywall screws. Use a 4-ft. level or a string stretched across the room to gauge whether the strips have any dips or humps. If necessary, use cedar shingles as shims between the furring and ceiling to straighten the furring.

2. Install cross blocks of furring between the long furring strips to support the joints at the ends of each panel. Toenail these blocks to the edges of the long strips using 6d or 8d finishing nails.

INSTALLING A TIN CEILING

project

Make a scale drawing of the ceiling on a piece of graph paper. After you have selected the pattern of your panels, draw the panel locations on your plan, centering the layout in the room. Divide any space that remains beyond that covered by the central field into two equal portions for the borders. For example, consider a room that is 15 x 15 feet, and assume that you will use panels with a 12-inch pattern and a cornice molding that projects 5 inches into the room. Subtracting the area covered by the molding leaves an exposed ceiling of 14 feet 2 inches x 14 feet 2 inches. If you can plan the main portion of the ceiling to be 12 feet square, it leaves 2 feet 2 inches (26 inches) for the border. Divide that dimension into two equal portions to leave a 13-inch-wide exposed border along each side of the room. The outer edge of the central ceiling panels will therefore be located 18 inches from the walls of the room (13-inch border + 5-inch cornice projection). Note: You could modify the layout in this room to yield either a wider or narrower border by changing the size of the central field.

TOOLS & MATERIALS
▎ Stud finder
▎ Drill/driver
▎ Drywall screws
▎ Plywood ½ in. thick
▎ Chalk-line box
▎ Ceiling panels
▎ Denatured alcohol (if needed)
▎ Leather work gloves
▎ Brad gun or hammer and cone-head nails
▎ Metal shears and tin snips
▎ Pliers
▎ Filler panels
▎ Cornice moldings
▎ Finishing nails

1 Use a stud finder to locate the ceiling joists. Place a mark on the ceiling near the wall to indicate the center of each joist; then snap a chalk line across the ceiling to clearly mark the joist positions. Next, use drywall screws to fasten sheets of ½-in.-thick construction-grade plywood to the joists, covering the entire ceiling. Make sure that the ends of the plywood sheets fall at the centerline of a joist, and stagger the sheets so that two adjacent sheets end on different joists.

2 Using your layout plan as a reference, snap chalk lines to indicate the outer edges of the main ceiling panels. Because the room dimensions may not be perfectly equal on opposite walls, the best way to approach this job is to find the center point of the ceiling along each wall and then measure ½ of the total dimension of the central field in opposite directions. *(continued on page 146)*

(continued from page 145)

3 If you're using unfinished steel panels, prepare the material by wiping the surfaces with denatured alcohol to remove any oils that might cause stains or contaminate the finish. Begin the panel installation at one corner of the room, aligning the panel edges with your chalk lines. The edges of metal panels can be quite sharp, so always wear leather gloves when handling the sheets to avoid cutting your hands.

4 A pneumatic brad gun is handy for fastening the metal panels to the plywood. Adjust the air pressure so that the heads of the brads are driven tight to the panel but do not push through. If you have a helper, you can hand nail the panels using cone-head nails. In either case, locate the nails every 6 in. along panel edges and down the center of the sheet. Most panels have small dimples to indicate the position of nails.

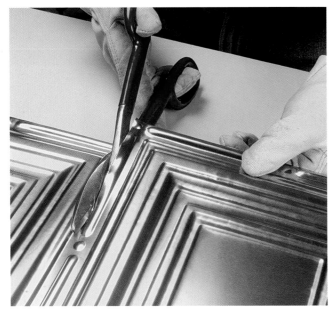

7 When panels must be cut, use metal shears to do the job. Sheets should always be cut between the decorative panel elements so that the design remains intact. Whenever possible, include the rounded and dimpled portion of the border to form an overlapping joint with the adjacent sheet. If cutting the sheet causes any distortion in the metal, you can use a pair of wide pliers to gently reshape the edge before installation.

8 If you plan to include lights in your ceiling, locate them in the center of a panel design; this may require you to have an electrician relocate existing wiring. Use a spare electrical junction box as a pattern to mark the required cutout on the metal surface.

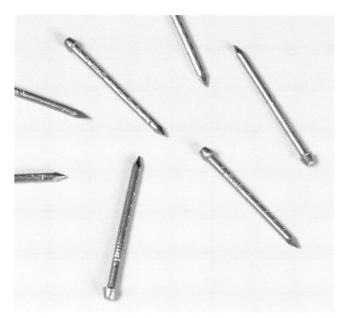

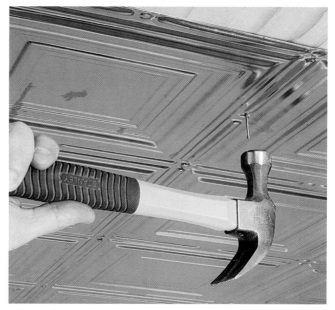

5 For hand-nailing metal sheets, use cone-head nails. Drive the nails so that the heads just rest against the surface of the sheet; use care to avoid causing any hammer marks or dents in the metal.

6 Ceiling panels are designed to overlap one another at seams. Drive nails through the double layer of metal to lock the panels together.

9 Drill a 1/2-in.-diameter hole just to the inside edge of the marked line; then use tin snips to make the cut-out, carefully following the layout line. Hold the panel in place on the ceiling to check that the opening aligns with the electrical box.

10 Filler panels are normally supplied in widths of 24 in., but they can be cut to size to accommodate your layout. You will find that it is easier to see the cut line if you place a strip of masking tape across the panel and mark it instead of the metal. Measure and mark the width of your border at each end of the panel; then use a straightedge guide to connect the marks.
(continued on page 148)

(continued from page 147)

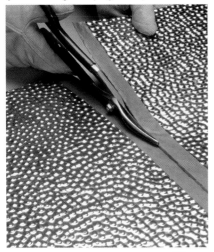

11 Use shears to cut the filler panel to the desired width. The material is quite flexible, so you should have no problems with distortion as you cut. Remember to wear leather gloves to protect your hands from the sharp edges.

12 Install the border sheets by nailing them to the plywood. Fillers should butt against the edges of the central ceiling panels, not overlap. These edges will be covered by molding, so you do not need to worry about tight joints. The same is true where the edge abuts the wall. Overlap adjacent sheets of filler by about 1/4 in.; drive nails through both sheets to seal the seams.

13 Flat molding is applied to cover the seams between the filler and main ceiling panels. Joints at the corners must be cut to form 45-deg. miters. To lay out these joints, place masking tape on the ends of the molding; then use an angle gauge as a guide to mark the cut lines.

17 Precut miters and copes are available for cornice molding, making the job much simpler. If possible, begin at an outside corner, holding the precut miter sections in place to check the fit of the joint. Use tin snips to make adjustments in the cut ends; then nail the sections in place. Nail the top edge of the molding to the plywood and the bottom edge to the wall studs.

18 Inside corner joints in cornice molding are treated much like those in wood moldings—they must be coped to fit tightly together. Precoped pieces are available for both left- and right-side joints. Begin the joint by running the first piece squarely into the corner so that it butts tightly to the end wall. Nail the top edge to the plywood substrate and the bottom edge to the wall studs.

19 Test the fit of the precut coped-end section against the installed cornice molding. The precut sections usually have small cuts directly into the end of the molding that allow you to bend it slightly to fit. If large gaps exist, you may need to recut the profile with tin snips. Once you are satisfied with the fit, nail the short section in place.

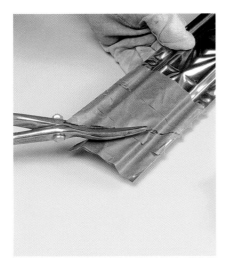

14 Use metal shears to cut the miter joints on the flat metal molding. Remove the masking tape, and use a pair of pliers to gently reshape the cut ends if they have been distorted.

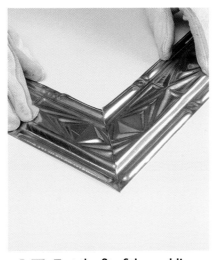

15 Test the fit of the molding corner joint before nailing either piece to the ceiling. If small adjustments are necessary, you can use a file to refine the joint.

16 The flat molding spans the joint between filler and main ceiling panels. The rounded edge of the molding should sit directly over the matching edge of the central panels. Nail through the edges to fasten the molding in place. Adjacent molding strips should overlap about $1/4$ in. at the end joints.

20 The technique of "caulking" is used to close open joints and ill-fitting seams. Use a hammer to gently tap the pointed end of a 16d common finishing nail, using the head end against the metal to coax the joint together. You can also use a small wood block or dowel instead of a nail.

21 Completed tin ceiling installation.

152 SOFFIT DESIGN

153 INSTALLING A SOFFIT

11 soffits

One of the more powerful ways you can change the sense of space in a room is to alter the shape of the ceiling surface. This may seem like a daunting proposition, but in fact, it can be one of the more approachable ceiling projects—the trick is to add a soffit around the room perimeter. While the definition of a soffit can vary with its particular application, in this instance it refers to an area of lowered ceiling adjacent to the walls in the room. You are probably most familiar with the concept as used in the kitchen, where a soffit often fills the space between the wall cabinets and ceiling. You can use the same basic technique to take a typical flat ceiling and transform it into a dynamic part of the overall design scheme. By providing new surfaces to emphasize the play of light and shadow, a soffit brings new energy to a room.

SOFFIT DESIGN

Soffits have the ability to create two distinct but related impressions. First, the areas of lowered ceiling tend to convey a feeling of increased intimacy and purpose; for instance, a soffit can be used to define an area for a specific use like a home office or TV nook. Second, by lowering the ceiling along the walls, even a small amount, the ceiling in the rest of the room is perceived as being higher than it actually is—the contrast between the different ceiling heights can be an effective architectural tool, actually changing how you experience the room.

Soffits can be constructed to be any height and depth, and they needn't be used along all walls in a room, or even the full length of a single wall. Although the illustrated project that follows suggests the construction of a soffit around an entire room, you should feel free to use the same techniques to create a design that suits your own needs. This is one tool that gives you complete flexibility in deciding how you want to change your ceiling.

■ **Practical Uses.** In addition to their function in modifying the shape of your ceiling, soffits have the added benefit of providing a way to hide some pretty ugly mechanical items such as pipes, ducts, and wires. While this

is most often an issue in a basement or utility room renovation, it can also come into play in the main rooms of a home, especially when new utilities are added to an older structure. For another option, you can add recessed lighting fixtures to a soffit—these can be tailored to a specific task, or they can provide ambient lighting for the room. While it would usually require cutting into the ceiling to run wires and install recessed fixtures, the soffit boxes allow you to easily add new lights with much less mess and minimal disruption of normal function.

One of the nice features of this type of project is that the materials required for construction are quite inexpensive. The framework for a soffit is usually built of 2x4 framing lumber or construction-grade plywood, and the finished surface is most often simple ½-inch-thick drywall. Of course, you have the option of applying other surface finishes to either the horizontal or vertical surfaces of a soffit; you could, for instance, apply wallpaper, boards, or tin ceiling panels to add another layer of detail or texture, or install a crown or bed molding at the points where the soffit joins the walls or ceiling.

ABOVE Soffits can house recessed lights as shown here or be used to hide cables, wiring, and heating ducts.

LEFT Soffits make the open section of a ceiling appear higher than it really is.

PREPARING RECESSED FIXTURES FOR SOFFITS

In most cases, the space inside a soffit frame is quite limited, giving you little room to maneuver. For this reason, you can save yourself quite a bit of aggravation by doing some prep work on your fixtures to get them ready for wiring before installing them. The fixture shown in the photos is a 4-inch-diameter recessed downlight, the kind used in the project on the following pages—keep in mind that each type of fixture will be slightly different in configuration, but the general requirements will be similar. Even if you do not feel confident to run the wires yourself, you can still save the electrician some work, and yourself some money, by following these simple steps.

Note: Whenever you plan to do any electrical work, be sure to research the local electrical code. If you have any questions as to the safety of a procedure or installation, you should consult a professional electrician to avoid creating an unsafe condition.

1 Each light comes equipped with an integral junction box that is intended to enclose the electrical connections between the house wiring and the fixture wires. Remove the access panel to expose the inside of the box. In this case, the panel is held in place by a simple spring clip.

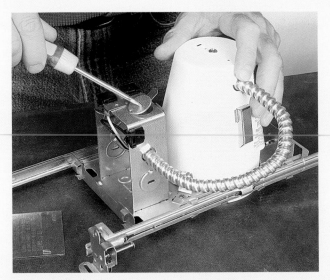

2 Use a slotted screwdriver to pry off one of the circular knockouts to allow the house wiring to enter the junction box. Most boxes are provided with two or three knockouts, but in most cases, you will only need to remove one.

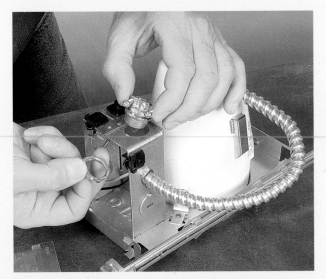

3 Install a cable connector that is appropriate to the type of electrical wiring that you will use. In some localities, the electrical code specifies that a particular type of wiring must be used (i.e., metal conduit). In the photo, a connector for nonmetallic cable is being installed. Regardless of the type of connector, place the body into the hole from the outside of the box, and thread on the fastening ring inside the box.

INSTALLING A SOFFIT

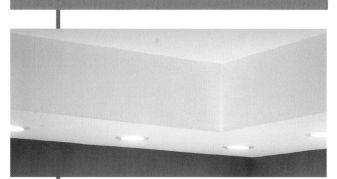

Some carpenters prefer to build soffits from construction-grade plywood and then sheath the surfaces with drywall. While this is certainly an acceptable approach, it can make it more difficult to run wires and install recessed light fixtures. To provide maximum flexibility, the alternative method is to assemble a framework of 2x2 and 2x4 lumber; this system allows you easy access to the interior of the soffit and makes it easy to add extra blocking to support hanging fixtures, if desired.

Before beginning actual construction, make a scale drawing of the room ceiling, including the new soffits. Use an electronic stud finder to locate the ceiling joists; mark the wall or ceiling adjacent to the intersecting walls to indicate the centerline of each joist.

The illustrated project includes the installation of recessed lighting fixtures—if you choose to install a soffit without any lighting, simply omit those steps.

TOOLS & MATERIALS
▮ Stud finder ▮ 2x2 and 2x4 lumber
▮ Chalk-line box ▮ Drill/driver ▮ Hammer
▮ Molly screws or toggle bolts ▮ Small level
▮ Recessed light fixture with mounting brackets
▮ Wiring and connectors for fixture
▮ Screwdriver ▮ Drywall
▮ Drywall saw ▮ Metal corner bead
▮ Drywall joint compound, tape, and taping tools

1 The vertical portion of the soffit is essentially a short 2x4 wall; the height equals the overall height of the soffit minus ½ in. (for drywall). For intersecting soffits, install double studs at the appropriate points to provide backing for the drywall at the inside corner and as a means of connecting the two soffit sections.

4 Where two soffits intersect, screw the two sections together to create a strong inside corner joint. Use a small "torpedo" level to check that the faces of the soffit sections remain plumb when you fasten them.

2 Establish chalk lines on the walls and ceiling to indicate the position of the outer edges of the soffit frame. These lines should be ½ in. inside the finished faces of the soffit to allow for the thickness of the drywall. Screw 2x2 blocking strips to the wall studs to form the back bottom edge of the soffit boxes. The distance from the ceiling to the bottom of these blocking strips should be equal to the height of the rough soffit faces.

3 Install the first soffit frame by screwing it to the ceiling joists. If your frame falls in a location where there are no joists, you can use hollow-wall anchors to hold the screws; for a small, lightweight soffit, spiral anchors will suffice, but for a large, heavy soffit, molly screws or toggle bolts are preferred.

5 Cut blocks of 2x4 lumber to form the bottom framework of the soffit. Mark the position of the blocks on the vertical soffit frames and on the blocking strips that are screwed to the wall. Toenail the blocks to both parts using 8d common nails. If you are planning to install recessed lighting fixtures in the soffit, make sure that the blocking does not interfere with the layout of the lights.

6 Once you have determined the desired spacing of the recessed light fixtures, mark those locations on the blocking strips and soffit face frames. Note: Most fixtures are mounted on adjustable brackets that will span openings up to 24 in.; if your soffit is wider than that dimension, you will need to install additional blocking to support the lights. Nail or screw the mounting brackets to the soffit framing. *(continued on page 156)*

(continued from page 155)

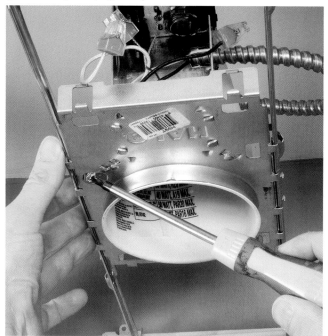

7 After the lights are fastened to the soffit, the fixture can still slide along the mounting rails. Move the body into the desired position, checking by measuring from the wall to the center of the fixture opening; then tighten the screw provided to lock it in place.

8 Run the wiring between fixtures before connecting the house wiring. You will have one wire bringing power into the fixture and another carrying power out to the next light. If you're using nonmetallic cable, you can place both wires through the same connector. Remove 4 or 5 in. of sheathing, and strip the wires to expose about ½ in. of the copper core. Tighten the screws on the connector to fix the cables to the junction box.

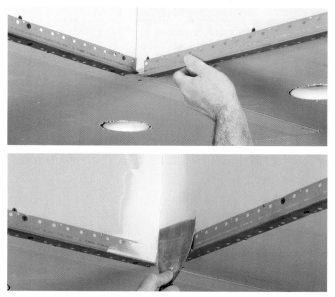

11 Lift the drywall panel into position, and fasten it to the soffit framing with drywall screws. Set the clutch on your driver so that the screw heads are set just below the surface of the drywall, creating a small dimple. Drive screws every 8 in. along the edges of the panel and into the intermediate blocking.

12 Install metal corner bead on all outside soffit edges (top). Use drywall screws to attach the bead to the framing. Cut the strips to length using metal shears. To finish an inside corner, begin by using a 3-in. drywall knife to spread compound on both surfaces (bottom).

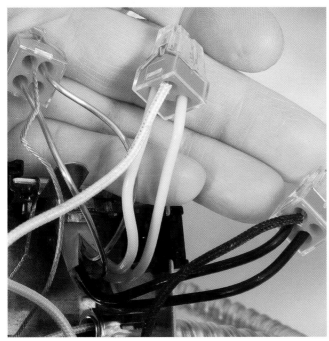

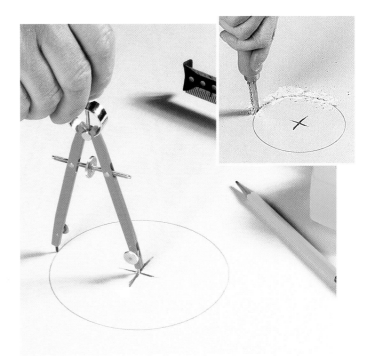

9 These fixtures use "push-in" connectors that eliminate the need for wire nuts. Simply push the exposed ends of the wires into the appropriate connector until it locks in place. Connect white wires to white wires, black wires to black wires, and copper ground connectors to each other. If you are not experienced in electrical work, hire an electrician to check your rough wiring and connect the circuits to the main house wiring.

10 Cut the drywall panels to cover the bottom surface of the soffit. If you have recessed lights in the soffit, carefully measure the locations of the center of each light, and transfer those dimensions to the drywall panel. Set a compass to draw a circle that is ¼ in. larger in diameter than the actual lights, and mark the outline of the cutouts on the drywall. Use a drywall saw to cut the openings for recessed light fixtures (inset).

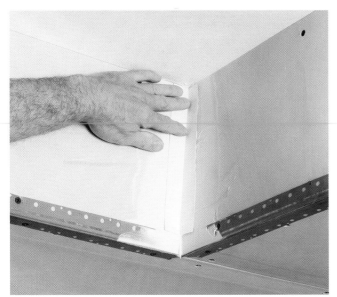

13 Cut a piece of drywall tape to length, and fold it lengthwise down the center to create a crease. Gently embed the tape into the compound; then use the drywall knife to smooth the tape. Cover one side of the tape with compound, and let it dry overnight before coating the second side. Lightly sand when dry. (See "Drywall Finishing," page 158.)

14 Install trim for light fixtures by pushing it into the housing until the clips snap into place. You will find a wide selection of trim ring styles, allowing you to tailor the look of the fixtures to suit your decor.

157

● DRYWALL FINISHING

The process of finishing drywall is essentially the same whether you are working on walls, ceilings, or soffits. The techniques are not particularly difficult, you just need to develop a "feel" for the material. Fortunately, it is easy, though messy, to sand away most mistakes, so you don't need to worry about learning on the job. Remember to always wear goggles and a proper dust mask when sanding drywall compound.

Finishing drywall is a multistep job, so banish any expectations that the first coat of compound will leave an attractive surface. A good job requires the application of multiple coats.

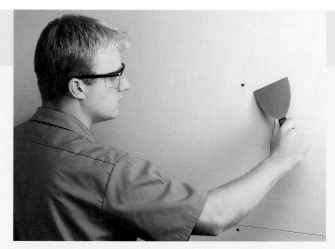

1 Check that all screws are properly set by sweeping a taping knife over the surface of the drywall. If you hear a "click" or feel any resistance, drive the screw further into the panel.

4 Cut a piece of paper joint tape to the appropriate length, and center it over the joint between the panels. Use gentle pressure to embed the tape into the compound.

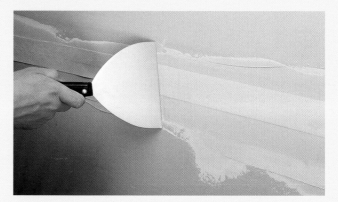

5 Make sure that the tape is fully embedded, checking for any air bubbles or spots that are not smooth. If necessary, peel the tape back and add compound to ensure a good bond. When the tape is smooth, apply a light coating of compound over it.

8 When dry, use a sanding block with 120-grit sand-paper to gently smooth the compound covering the drywall screws. As your technique improves, you will find that only light sanding is required between coats.

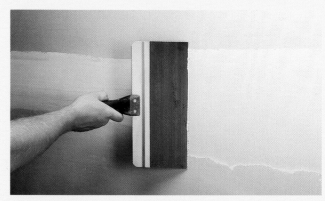

9 Use a 10-in. blade to apply the first top coat of drywall compound. The goal is to have the edges of the compound blend into the surrounding surface.

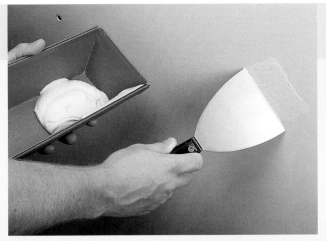

2 Use a 3-in.-wide drywall knife to spread compound over the recessed fasteners. Drywall compound shrinks slightly as it dries, so you can expect to fill these holes more than once.

3 Where two panels meet, use a 3-in. knife to spread compound directly over the joint, pressing a bit to force it into the gap.

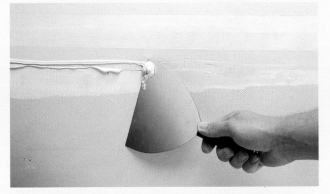

6 To avoid excessive sanding, use the edge of the blade to scrape away ridges of excess compound at the edges of a seam.

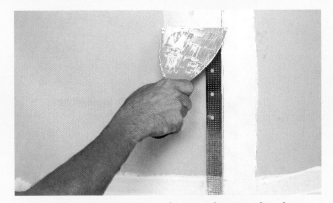

7 Apply compound over the metal corner beads at outside corners. Bridge the knife between the wall and the raised edge of the bead. This will allow just enough compound to cover the body of the bead.

10 Use a pole sander to ease the job of sanding long seams and overhead areas. Always use light pressure when sanding so that you do not abrade the paper drywall surface.

11 Apply the second and final topcoat: a 12-in.-wide coat over the joints. Smooth the middle first; then smooth each edge. Clean the knife on the edge of the pan after each pass. Sand all joints smooth.

162 BEAM DESIGNS

164 INSTALLING BEAMS

12 beam ceilings

A beamed ceiling is often a defining architectural feature in a room—the first thing that you notice upon entering, and something that continues to draw your attention when other elements drift into the background of your consciousness. Because decorative beams derive from their structurally necessary cousins, their use automatically conveys notions of strength and solidity. Beams can take many forms, and they can be used in a variety of decorating styles; at one extreme, rough, hand-hewn, or distressed beams might be appropriate for a casual family room, while polished hardwood beams could easily enhance a formal dining room or library.

BEAM DESIGNS

While the visual impact of a beamed ceiling is considerable, the techniques that are required for installation are relatively straightforward, and this type of project is definitely within the reach of someone with moderate carpentry skills. You can easily tailor the design, material, and construction details to suit your taste, budget, and level of experience.

■ **Beam Layout.** The size and spacing of beams on a ceiling should be appropriate to the size and height of the room. In general, larger rooms with taller ceilings can tolerate larger beams that are more closely spaced than small rooms with low ceilings. Similarly, the materials or finish of the beams will affect their impact on the room design. Beams that are painted the same color as the ceiling will be less imposing than those that are painted a contrasting color or receive a stained or clear finish. Because beams fall into the category of architectural trim, it is a natural and safe option to use the same material or finish that is featured on the other trim features in a room, such as baseboards and casing—this treatment can tie the elements together to form a cohesive design theme.

Ceiling beams typically run parallel with one another and can be placed a uniform distance apart or with varied spacing. In most cases, when a beam runs directly along a wall, a half-beam is constructed, creating the illusion that the remainder of the beam is buried in the wall structure. Beams can be terminated directly at the wall surface, but you can also fabricate half-beams along the end walls that serve as the terminal points of the central beams; when using this type of design, the half-beams can be made larger or deeper to suggest support for the smaller, intersecting members. For a simpler approach, you can mount a wide frieze board on the walls and allow the beams to end against this surface. This solution has some distinct advantages because it provides a clean transition between the beam and walls and eliminates the awkward task of fitting prebuilt beams between the drywall surfaces.

■ **Nonstructural Beams.** Decorative beams are typically built-up U-shaped forms attached to the ceiling with blocking strips. The simplest approach to beam design will use stock lumber sizes for the sides and bottoms of the structure, but you needn't feel locked into these dimensions. If you have access to a table saw, you can eas-

ily trim the individual elements to any size you desire.

You can install beams to run either parallel with or perpendicular to the direction of the ceiling joists in a room. If the beams run parallel with the joists, you can definitely fasten the blocking strips directly to the joists. It's possible to lay out the beams so that each falls directly beneath a joist, but this limits the placement options. When a beam must be placed in a spot where there is no framing member for attachment, you can use hollow-wall anchors to hold the blocking to the ceiling surface. For a more drastic alternative, you can open up the ceiling to reveal

the framing, and then install solid blocking between the joists to support the beams. This should only be necessary if the beams are especially large and heavy. Regardless of the beam layout, it is always best to begin by determining the direction and location of the ceiling joists in the room. Use an electronic stud finder to locate the joists, placing a light pencil mark to indicate the joist center on the ceiling adjacent to the intersecting wall. Then you can use a chalk line to connect the marks on opposite sides of the room to provide a clear map of the joist layout.

Beams can be constructed in different styles and using a variety of techniques. Beam bottoms can be either flush to the sides or recessed to create a shadow line. The joint between the sides and bottom may be square, or shaped to a rounded or chamfered profile. The sides of the beams can be constructed of flat lumber or molded stock, such as baseboard, or apply molding over the flat sides to add detail. At the junction of beam and ceiling, you have the option of creating a clean, square joint between the sides and ceiling, or applying a sprung or flat molding to further embellish the design.

LEFT To unify a design, use the same finish found on other trimwork in the room.

BELOW Rough-hewn beams add a distinctive rustic touch to a room.

INSTALLING BEAMS

While it is possible to build beams in place, one board at a time, it's usually much simpler to prefabricate the beams and then hang them on the ceiling; this is the system illustrated in the photos. And while it is also possible to simply assemble the parts with nails and glue, the use of joining plates makes the job much easier and also yields better results. Joining plates not only reinforce the joints between the beam parts, but they serve as registration aides that automatically position the parts in relation to one another.

In this project, the sides of the beams extend ¼ inch below the bottoms. If you decide to use a different beam design, you will need to make appropriate modifications in layout and construction technique.

TOOLS & MATERIALS
- ▌ Measuring tape
- ▌ Chalk-line box ▌ Stud finder
- ▌ Lumber for blocking strips
- ▌ Screws, hollow-wall anchors
- ▌ Plate joiner ▌ Shims
- ▌ Glue ▌ Clamps
- ▌ Hammer or nail gun
- ▌ Finishing nails
- ▌ Lumber for finished beams
- ▌ Stain or paint
- ▌ Molding (optional)

1 Carefully measure and mark the locations of blocking strips for the beams and half-beams; then snap chalk lines to indicate the position of the strip edges. For a clean and accurate mark, stretch the string between the layout marks; lift it perpendicular to the plane of the wall or ceiling; and let it snap against the surface only once.

5 Place matching marks every 6 to 8 in. on the inside surfaces of beam sides and bottoms to indicate the centers of joining plates. While it is not necessary to use joining plates for beam construction, it does make assembly much easier and also reinforces the joints.

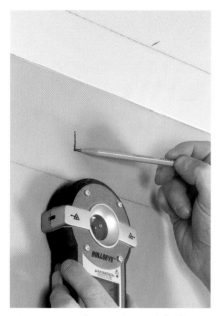

2 Use an electronic stud finder to locate the centerlines of studs and ceiling joists. Place a pencil mark to indicate the center of each intersecting framing member near the previously established chalk lines.

3 Use 2x2 lumber for blocking strips for half-beams that run along perimeter walls. Screw the strips into wall studs and ceiling joists. If there are no framing members to use for fastening, use hollow-wall anchors to attach the strips.

4 Attach blocking strips for the central beams to the ceiling joists. The strips should be the same width as the bottom panels of the beams. Use either two-by framing lumber or $5/4$ common pine for these strips—either will provide adequate nailing for hanging the beams.

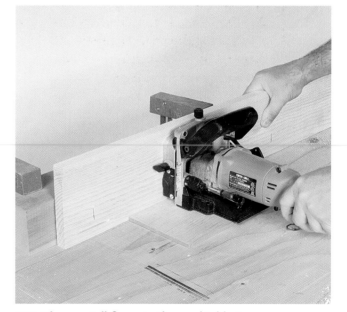

6 Place a beam bottom panel flat on the worktable surface, with its inside face up, to cut joining plate slots in its edge. Hold both the plate joiner and bottom tightly to the table so that the slots will all be cut at a uniform height.

7 Clamp a tall fence to the worktable to use as a backer for cutting joining-plate slots in the face of the beam sides. Hold one of the sides against the fence with its bottom edge flat on the worktable top. Place a $1/4$-in.-thick shim under the plate joiner while you cut the slots. This system will guarantee that the sides extend exactly $1/4$-in. below the bottom of the beam.

(continued on page 166)

(continued from page 165)

8 Place a small bead of glue in each joining plate slot; then lightly spread glue on both sides of each plate before slipping it into its slot. You will find it easier to install the plates in the beam sides, rather than the edges of the bottom, because the slots are more accessible when the parts are laid flat.

9 Assemble the sides to the bottom panel. If you have adequate clamps, you can avoid using any other mechanical fasteners—simply apply a clamp every 8 to 10 in. down the beam to squeeze the joints tight. Allow the glue to set for at least 30 minutes before removing the clamps.

12 Begin the installation by lifting the preassembled half-beams into position. The inside face of the beam side should rest against the blocking strip mounted to the ceiling, and the bottom should rest against the strip mounted to the wall.

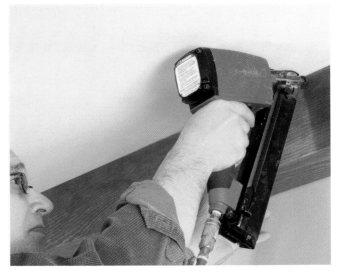

13 Drive finishing nails through the beam side to fasten it to the blocking strip on the ceiling. Drive nails through the beam bottom to fasten it to the blocking strip on the wall.

10 If you do not have clamps, use nails to hold the parts together. Drive 8d finishing nails or 2½-in. gun nails through the sides into the edges of the bottom (top). Set the nailheads below the wood surface. If you are unable to construct the beams in a single piece, build the sections with staggered joints as shown in the photo (bottom). Fasten the two parts together by nailing through the sides into the extended bottom "tongue."

11 Sand the outer surfaces of the beams to remove scratches and mill marks (top). Use the finest grit that will easily remove the defects—in most cases 120-grit paper is appropriate. Apply the final finish before installation (bottom). Any minor scratches or nailholes can be filled after installation. If your beams will be painted the same color as the ceiling, you might choose to wait until installation is complete for the final coat.

14 Lift the central beams so that they slip over the mounting strips on the ceiling. The top edges of the beam should rest against the drywall surface. Drive finishing nails through the sides of the beam to fasten it to the blocking strip.

15 Many designs add molding between the beams and ceiling; the molding serves two purposes. First, the trimwork can hide any gaps between the two elements that result from uneven or damaged ceilings and walls. Second, the molding adds another dimension to the beams, providing a more layered and eye-catching design. Use standard techniques—coped, mitered, and scarf joints—to install the trimwork.

170 COFFERED DESIGNS

172 INSTALLING A COFFERED CEILING

13 coffered ceilings

If you've had the chance to visit or view pictures of some of the grand homes, churches, and palaces of Europe, you know that coffered ceilings have a long and storied history. While coffered ceilings may have originated as an engineering tool, to lighten and support a ceiling structure, this architectural feature was soon identified with elegance and luxury. The ceilings that you will find in historic European buildings are often opulent examples of the decorative arts, with gold leaf and scenic paintings freely used as embellishments. But if you look beyond the surface, the same basic concept that underlies these highly wrought ceilings can be applied in your own home to add character and elegance to a room.

COFFERED DESIGNS

A coffered ceiling consists of a series of recessed areas, called coffers, separated by intersecting beams. Coffers are most often square or rectangular, but you will also see ceilings that feature other shapes like octagons or diamonds—these are defined by beams that intersect at angles other than 90 degrees. Although the shape of the coffers is one dominant feature of the ceiling, the materials and finishes used can add considerably to its overall effect.

At one end of the decorative spectrum, you can create a coffered ceiling with beams of drywall or plaster, covering the surfaces with paint or wallpaper. These treatments can be very simple, using a single color, or very elaborate, using multiple colors, decorative painting techniques, or highly figured wall coverings. Another choice would be to use wooden beams to define the coffers. Once again, these can be simple or ornate, painted or finished with stain and varnish. And regardless of the material used for the beams, the ceiling surfaces in the coffers can receive a variety of finishes including paint, leather, wallpaper, fabric, tin ceiling panels, or veneers. Of course, any ceiling treatment should be consistent with the prevailing design scheme in the room.

Keep in mind that any coffered ceiling, no matter how simple, is a serious design statement. This type of project is usually most appropriate for the more formal rooms of the home, such as the living room, dining room, or library. But if carefully considered, you can also use the concept in a kitchen, family room, or bedroom.

Design Considerations

As with any architectural feature, it is important that you design a coffered ceiling so that its elements are appropriate to the scale of the room. Of course, there is no firm rule or formula that you need to follow, but you should carefully consider the size of the room and height of the ceiling when devising your plan. As a general guide, larger rooms with taller ceilings can accept coffers that are large—divided by deeper and wider beams—proportions that might overpower a small space with low ceilings. These decisions can be further affected by the finish that you ultimately plan for the ceiling, as a monochromatic or simple treatment is less imposing than a contrasting, highly figured, or ornate surface that draws your attention.

You can also entertain the possibility of mixing beams of different width and/or depth to divide the coffers.

OPPOSITE The size of the beams and the coffers should correspond to the ceiling height in the room.

ABOVE This timber-frame structure allows for a small coffered area in the kitchen.

Often beams of larger size are run in one direction to create the illusion of supporting timbers, with smaller beams running between them to separate the individual coffers.

■ **Planning.** After you have a rough idea of the elements you want to include in your ceiling design, the next step is to develop an exact layout. Begin by making a scale drawing of the room ceiling on a piece of graph paper. Make trial drawings of different coffer layouts to find one that suits you. While you will find many ceilings that have coffers that are all of equal size, this is certainly not necessary. For example, in a dining room, it is common to have a single large coffer centered over the table with smaller coffers on the rest of the ceiling.

In most cases, a half-beam or wide frieze is installed around the perimeter of the room to accept the ends of the main beams. To arrive at the final coffer measurements, add the width of all beams down the length of the room, including half-beams at the end walls; then subtract that total from the overall dimension. Divide the remainder by the number of coffers to find the coffer length. Repeat the process for the width of the room.

INSTALLING A COFFERED CEILING

project

Make the project shown here with materials that you can find in any home center or lumberyard. In this design, beams of uniform depth and width intersect at right angles to form square (or rectangular) coffers; half-beams of the same depth surround the room, providing a simple transition between the ceiling and wall surfaces.

A layered grid provides support for rough coffers that you can build in your home workshop. By constructing the grid in two layers, you eliminate the need to open the ceiling to install extra blocking between ceiling joists. This system uses inexpensive common-grade pine lumber as the foundation for a finished ceiling of red oak. The bottom surfaces of the beams are designed to make the most economical use of standard width lumber—1x4 and 1x6 boards. Two separate molding profiles are included in the design—a standard colonial baseboard molding is used to form the sides of the beams, and a traditional crown molding provides a graceful transition between the beams and coffer surface. You also have the option of covering the actual ceiling surfaces with a veneered panel (as shown), using another type of material to cover the coffer, or simply painting the drywall and leaving the ceiling surface exposed.

TOOLS & MATERIALS
▌ Stud finder ▌ Chalk-line box
▌ Table saw ▌ Lumber for blocking
▌ Drill/Driver ▌ Screws
▌ 1x6 pine for coffer boxes
▌ Plywood for corner braces
▌ Shims ▌ 1x4 oak
▌ 1x6 oak ▌ Hammer or nail gun
▌ Finishing nails or brads
▌ ¼-in.-thick red oak plywood
▌ Construction adhesive
▌ Baseboard and crown molding

1 Begin the layout of your project by marking the center of each ceiling joist near the intersecting walls, and snapping a chalk line to connect these marks. Next, use the chalk line to mark the outer edges of the blocking strips along the walls and ceiling. Plan to install the first layer of blocking strips perpendicular to the ceiling joists—with this system you will maximize the solid points of attachment for the blocking and will minimize the need for hollow-wall anchors.

3 Begin by installing blocking strips directly to ceiling joists and wall studs to form backing for the half beams. If you encounter any spots where there are no framing members for fastening, use hollow-wall anchors to hold the screws. Next, screw the first layer of blocking strips to the ceiling joists, aligning the edges with the previously established layout lines.

2 Because it is necessary to use materials of nonstandard widths for the ceiling, you will need to rip lumber to size. Use a table saw to trim blocking strips to the required dimension. If you do not have access to a saw, you can assemble a cut list and have your millwork supplier trim the stock to size. Here common-grade pine is ripped for blocking—you can also use two-by framing lumber, but it is heavier and more likely to be warped or bowed. (Saw guard removed for clarity of photo.)

4 Mark the positions of the second layer of blocking strips on the first layer. You can speed the process and guarantee uniformity by making gauge strips from scrap lumber, plywood, or hardboard. If your ceiling requires more than one size coffer, simply make a gauge strip to correspond to each measurement.

5 Screw the second layer of blocking strips to those strips already fastened to the ceiling. If you use pine lumber for blocking, the soft nature of the wood makes pilot holes for the screws unnecessary.
(continued on page 174)

(continued from page 173)

6 Completed grid of blocking strips, ready for rough coffer installation.

9 Make a corner brace from scrap plywood, and temporarily screw it to one of the coffer corners to hold the box square while it is installed. You needn't make braces for every box because you can remove and reuse the braces after each box is installed.

10 To provide an easy way to support the box during installation, screw a piece of 1x2 lumber across the bottom edges of the box to use as a handle. Begin installation of the coffers by lifting the first box into position in one of the grid openings. Push it up so that the top edges of the box are flush against the ceiling surface.

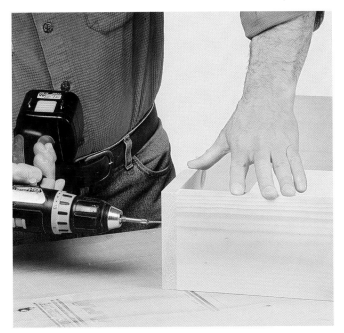

7 Rip and crosscut 1x6 common pine to size for the coffer boxes. Use a table saw, radial-arm saw, or sliding compound miter saw to make the end cuts to ensure that they are square. Assemble the boxes by screwing the corners together using drywall screws.

8 Check that the each coffer box is square. You can use a framing square to check the corners, but if the sides are even slightly bowed this can be unreliable. For an alternative method, compare opposite diagonal measurements (shown); if the measurements are equal, the box is square.

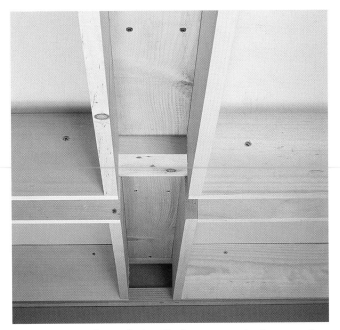

11 Attach the coffers by driving screws through the sides into the edges of the blocking strips. Because the strips sit at different heights, you will need to adjust the location of the screws accordingly. If you find that the coffer box is loose in the grid opening, you can place thin shims between the outer box surface and blocking strips; try to make sure that the box is centered in the grid opening.

12 View of installed coffer boxes. For the best results, you should try to align the edges of the coffer boxes in each row. (continued on page 176)

(continued from page 175)

13 Cut a flat miter on the end of 1x4 stock to form an inside corner for the bottom of one of the half-beams. Nail the piece to the blocking strip along the wall and to the bottom edges of the coffer boxes. Note that the exposed edge of the red oak 1x4 should be flush with the inside edge of the coffer box. If there is a small space between the oak bottom and the wall, you can either install molding to cover the joint or apply a small bead of caulk to fill the gap.

16 Cut short pieces of 1x6 to form the perpendicular beam bottoms. These pieces should be cut for a snug fit so that you do not have any noticeable gaps in the joints. Nail them to the coffer boxes.

14 Cut a matching flat miter on the adjacent piece of oak 1x4 to form the inside corner joint for the half-beam. Test the fit; make any necessary adjustments; then nail it in place.

15 Cut 1x6 oak stock to length to form beam bottoms that extend the length of the room. If you do not have stock long enough to span the entire distance, cut a tight butt joint to join the pieces. Nail the stock in place, driving the fasteners into the bottom edges of the coffer boxes.

17 It is likely that not all of the beam bottom pieces will align perfectly—this can be due to an uneven ceiling surface or boards of varying thickness. You can fix minor problems by driving shims between the bottom edges of the coffer boxes and the beam bottom boards; small cedar shingles, often used for trim installations, are perfect for this application. Score the shingle along the in-side edge of the coffer, and snap off the excess.

18 If you wish to cover the ceiling with a wooden surface, you can use ¼-in.-thick red oak plywood with one good face. This material is quite inexpensive and provides a lightweight and attractive solution. Cut the panels to fit within the coffer boxes—you can make them ¼ in. smaller than the opening—then apply construction adhesive to the top surface of the panel before lifting it into position. *(continued on page 178)*

(continued from page 177)

19 Press the plywood panels to the ceiling to allow the construction adhesive to form a good bond; then drive brads around the perimeter of the panel to hold it in place. Remember to arrange the panels so that the grain is oriented in the same direction.

22 Cut a coped profile on one end of the second piece of molding and a square cut on the opposite end. Use this technique for both the second and third pieces of base.

23 The last piece of molding in each coffer requires two coped ends, but this is a particularly tricky task, especially for a novice. Fortunately, there is a simple way around this predicament—simply divide the molding into two separate pieces and join them in the center with a scarf joint.

20 Place gauge marks in the corners of the coffer boxes, along the edges of the beam bottoms, to indicate the bottom edge of the inverted oak base stock. You can eliminate the need for individual measurements by making a simple marking jig. Just screw two pieces of scrap lumber together with their ends offset by $^3/_8$ in. Hold the gauge against the beam bottom, and mark along the top edge.

21 The exposed beam sides are formed from inverted base molding. To achieve a tight fit at the corners, it is best to use traditional base installation techniques—the only difference is that the molding is upside down. This means that you should cut coped joints at the inside corners. Begin by cutting square ends on the first piece so that its ends fit tightly against the rough coffer box sides. Fasten it in place with brads.

24 Finish each coffer by installing crown molding between the base and the plywood ceiling panels. Once again, use coped joints at inside corners.

25 Completed coffered ceiling.

This list of manufacturers and associations is meant to be a general guide to additional industry and product-related sources. It is not intended as a listing of products and manufacturers represented by the photographs in this book.

A & M Wood Specialty
357 Eagle St. N.
P.O. Box 32040
Cambridge, Ontario N3H 5M2
Canada
800-265-2750
www.forloversofwood.com
Domestic and exotic hardwood lumber and veneers—shipping available. Milling, jointing, and planing services.

The American Tin Ceiling Company
1825 60th Place E.
Bradenton, FL 34203
888-231-7500
www.americantinceilings.com
Tin ceiling panels including drop-in panels for suspended ceiling systems.

Armstrong World Industries, Inc.
P.O. Box 3001
Lancaster, PA 17604
800-233-3823
www.armstrong.com
Manufacturer of ceiling tiles, planks, and suspended ceiling systems.

Balmer Architectural Mouldings
271 Yorkland Blvd.
Toronto, Ontario M2J 1S5
Canada
800-665-3454
www.balmer.com
Supplier of polyurethane and plaster moldings, medallions, and domes.

Bradbury & Bradbury
P.O. Box 155
Benicia, CA 94510
707-746-1900
www.bradbury.com
Handprinted wall and ceiling papers in historically accurate patterns. Design services available.

Carter & Company
Mt. Diablo Handprints
451 Ryder St.
Vallejo, CA 94590
707-554-2682
www.carterandco.com
Handprinted historic wallpaper.

Chelsea Decorative Metal Company
8212 Braewick Dr.
Houston, TX 77074
713-721-9200
www.thetinman.com
Tin ceiling supplies.

Classic Ceilings
902 E. Commonwealth Ave.
Fullerton, CA 92831
800-992-8700
www.classicceilings.com
Tin ceiling supplies.

Decorators Supply Corp.
3610 S. Morgan St.
Chicago, IL 60609
773-847-6300
www.decoratorssupply.com
Plaster moldings and medallions.

Fypon
960 W. Barre Rd.
Archbold, OH 43502
800-446-3040
www.fypon.com
Urethane medallions and domes.

Historic Houseparts, Inc.
540 South Ave.
Rochester, NY 14620
888-558-2329
www.historichouseparts.com
Ceiling medallions.

Home Depot
800-430-3376
For store locations see
www.homedepot.com
General building supplies, millwork, ceiling tiles, suspended ceiling systems.

Lowe's
800-445-6937
For store locations see
www.lowes.com
*General building supplies, lumber,
millwork, drywall, ceiling tiles,
suspended ceiling systems, finishes,
tools, and hardware.*

Ornamental Mouldings
3894 Comanche Rd.
P.O. Box 4068
Archdale, NC 27263
800-779-1135
www.ornamental.com
*Wood moldings and architectural
ornaments.*

Rockler Woodworking and Hardware
4365 Willow Dr.
Medina, MN 55340
800-279-4441
www.rockler.com
*Woodworking tools and supplies,
hardware.*

Royal Design Studio
3517 Main St., Suite 302
Chula Vista, CA 91911
800-747-9767
www.royaldesignstudio.com
Stencil supplies and tools.

San Francisco Victoriana, Inc.
2070 Newcomb Ave.
San Francisco, CA 94124
415-648-0313
www.sfvictoriana.com
*Extensive line of stock molding profiles,
including traditional Victorian trim
elements and custom molding services.*

Wallpapers Plus
9 Pheasant Ln.
Minneapolis, MN 55127
888-242-7448
www.wallpapersplus.com
*Wallpapers, including Lincrusta and
Anaglypta.*

**White River Hardwoods
Woodworks, Inc.**
1197 Happy Hollow Rd.
Fayetteville, AR 72701
800-558-0119
www.mouldings.com
*Hardwood and resin moldings, includ-
ing flexible moldings. Carved architectural ornaments and custom molding.*

Wishihadthat, Inc.
2841 Unicorn Rd., Suite 101
Bakersfield, CA 93308
800-419-1130
www.wishihadthat.com
*Medallions, domes, moldings, and
ceiling tiles.*

Woodcraft
P.O. Box 1686
Parkersburg, WV 26102
800-225-1153
www.woodcraft.com
Woodworking tools.

Base (or baseboard) Trim members mounted to the bottom of a wall, that cover the gap between the wall and floor. Base profiles are often inverted for use as a frieze in cornice trim.

Base cap Molding that is intended to cover the top edge of base trim. Base cap profiles are frequently used as parts of compound cornice assemblies.

Beam A horizontal structural member, typically used to support a floor or ceiling. Beamed ceilings are decorative features meant to mimic the appearance of structural beams.

Bevel An angled cut, other than 90 degrees, into the thickness of a piece of stock and with the grain.

Casing A flat or profiled piece of trim that is most often used to surround a door or window opening. Casing profiles are also used in cornices and applied molding installations on ceilings and walls.

Caulk A flexible material that is used to fill gaps and seams between adjacent materials. Caulk is supplied in tubes that require an inexpensive gun applicator to transfer it to the target area.

Chair rail A horizontal band of trim, usually located between 30 and 36 inches from the floor. Chair rails were originally intended to protect the wall surface from damage, but now function more as a decorative feature. Molding profiles that are designed as chair rails can also be used in built-up cornice trim.

Chalk line A string covered with powdered chalk used to mark a straight line between distant points. A chalk-line box opens to

accept the powdered chalk and has a reel inside that allows you to automatically spread chalk on the line as it extends from the box.

Coffer A recessed area in a ceiling that is defined by intersecting beams. The surface of a coffer can be painted or covered with wallpaper or a veneered panel.

Coped joint A wood joint in which the end of one piece is cut to match the face profile of the adjacent stock.

Coping saw A handsaw with a thin blade held taut between the ends of a C-shaped frame. The name of the saw comes from its frequent use to make the intricate cuts

required for "coped," or fitted, inside corner joints on molding stock.

Corner bead Metal or plastic trim used to finish outside corners of drywall surfaces.

Cornice A molding or assembly of moldings at the junction of walls and ceiling.

Cove A concave profile on a molding.

Crosscut To cut a board perpendicular to the direction of the wood grain.

Crown molding A molding designed to sit at an angle between the wall and ceiling. Crown moldings can also be used as capitals on

glossary

square columns or to wrap around the head casing in traditional door trim.

Dome A modification to a ceiling that exhibits an arched shape. True domes require reconfiguration of the ceiling framework, while surface domes can be mounted directly on a flat ceiling surface.

Drywall A sheet composed of a gypsum core covered with heavy paper, which is used to form the interior surface of walls and ceilings.

Finger-joint A means of joining short lengths of lumber together to form a long board or piece of molding stock. Interlocking fingers are cut in the matching ends and the parts are glued together. Finger-jointed stock is suitable only for paint-grade applications.

Frieze A horizontal band of decoration that runs along the wall of a room, usually just under the ceiling. A frieze can also be the area of a wall between the picture molding and cornice or can be an integral part of a cornice assembly.

Grain The pattern of the fibers in wood that is a result of the growth of the tree. Typically, the grain direction runs along the length of a board. The appearance of grain in a board is largely determined by the way it is cut relative to the annual growth rings of the tree.

Hardwood Wood that comes from a deciduous tree—one that loses its leaves in winter. Common species include oak, maple, cherry, birch, and walnut.

Joining plate Football-shaped wafers of compressed wood that fit in

matching semicircular slots in a wood joint. Plates are available in a range of sizes for different applications.

Joint compound Premixed gypsum based material with the consistency of thick paste, used to fill seams and fastener holes in drywall panels.

Joist A horizontal member in house framing that supports a floor or ceiling.

Level A term used to describe a perfectly horizontal surface. Also a tool used to determine whether a surface is level or plumb.

MDF Medium-density fiberboard. A manufactured material consisting of fine wood fibers bonded with glue under heat and pressure. MDF is used for panel stock as well as moldings and columns.

Medallion A molded embellishment, most often of plaster, fiberglass, or polyurethane, applied to the ceiling. Medallions can be found in different shapes—round, square, rectangular, or oval.

Millwork A descriptive term used to describe various manufactured wooden trim components, such as lumber, moldings, doors, railings, columns, and architectural ornaments.

Miter An angled cut into the face of a piece of stock, across the grain, for a woodworking joint. Typically, the angle of a miter cut is equal to one-half of the total angle of the joint.

Miter saw A saw used to make angled cuts for woodworking joints. Hand-operated and power models are available, as well as models with sliding heads for wide, compound angle cuts.

Molding Decorative strips of wood, composite, or synthetic materials that are used in various trim applications.

Nail set A pointed metal tool used to drive the heads of finishing nails below the wood surface. Sets are available in various sizes to match nailhead diameter.

Ogee A molding shape that follows an S-shaped double curve. Based on the Greek cyma recta moldings, the profile is concave at the top and convex at the bottom.

Panel molding A variety of molding profiles most often used to create or embellish panels on either flat or recessed surfaces. These moldings are commonly used on doors, architectural paneling, mantles, and cornice assemblies.

Picture rail A molding with a rounded, protruding top edge designed to be mounted high on the walls of a room. The edge accepts hooks for hanging pictures.

Plate joiner A power tool that cuts semicircular slots in wood to accept compressed wood plates for joining parts. A plate joiner has an adjustable fence that aids in positioning the slot relative to a board surface, as well as various depth stops for different size joining plates.

Plumb A term used to describe a perfectly vertical surface.

Purlin A horizontal roof beam that supports the rafters.

Rasp A metal tool with a rough, toothed surface used for rapid removal of wood. Rasps are available in flat and shaped models, as well as in various tooth-size configurations.

Rip To cut a board parallel with the direction of the wood grain.

Router A power tool that consists of a motor with tool-holding collet held in a portable base. Various cutting tools can be mounted to the end of the rotating shaft for grooving and shaping wood.

Sandpaper Paper or cloth that is coated with an abrasive grit, used to smooth wood surfaces. Sandpaper is graded by the size and type of grit and the weight of the backer. Higher numbers indicate finer abrasive.

Scarf joint A joint that is used to join two boards or moldings end to end. Overlapping bevel cuts are made in the two parts so that, when assembled, the joint appears invisible.

Shim A strip of wood that is used to fill a gap behind a structural or trim item. Most often, narrow tapered shingles are used for this purpose.

Skylight A glass or acrylic window mounted in the roof to provide natural light to a room. Some skylights are fixed, and others can be opened for ventilation.

Soffit An area of dropped ceiling adjacent to the walls in a room. Also, the exposed, horizontal underside of an overhead building component, such as a cornice, arch, balcony, or eave.

Spring angle A pair of angles that explains the way that a crown molding intersects the planes of ceiling and wall. The first number corresponds to the angle between ceiling and the back of the molding, and the second is the angle between the wall and back of the molding.

Square A primary concept in carpentry—that two surfaces are perpendicular, or at 90 degrees to one another. Also, the steel tool used to mark square lines or test that two surfaces are square.

Stencil A template used to draw or paint a repeating pattern on a surface such as a wall or ceiling. Manufactured stencils are often made of plastic or polyester film, but a wide variety of materials can be used, including cardboard, paper, vinyl, and linoleum.

Stud Vertical structural members in house framing, typically of 2x4 or 2x6 lumber.

Toenail To drive a nail at an angle, through one framing member and into another, to lock the parts together.

Tray ceiling A decorative ceiling treatment that features a sloped, stepped, or curved transition between the walls and ceiling. The name derives from the idea that the ceiling resembles an inverted tray.

Veneer A thin layer of wood that is sawn or sliced from a log. Inexpensive veneers can be glued together to form plywood, often with a valuable lumber species displayed on the outer surfaces. Veneers can also be applied to composite cores such as MDF and particleboard.

Wall frames Assemblies of panel molding applied to a drywall or plaster wall for decorative purposes.

Warp A term indicating that a board is bowed or is not flat.

index

A

www.abbingdon.com, 23
Accent lighting, 21
Acoustic tiles, 18, 28–29, 43
    tools for, 42–43
Alcoves, dropped, 28
Ambient lighting, 21
www.americanceilings.com, 23
American Tile Ceiling Co., 18
Anaglypta, 12
Angle, bisecting, 48
Angle gauge, 47
Architectural styles
    Art Deco, 70, 142
    Art Nouveau, 70
    Arts and Crafts style, 27, 70, 104
    Georgian, 27, 104
    Victorian, 23, 27, 70, 104, 142
Armstrong (www.armstrong.com), 19
Art Deco style, 70, 142
Articulating ladder, 39
Art Nouveau, 70
Arts and Crafts style, 27, 70, 104
Asbestos, 18
Assembly jig, constructing, 88

B

Back-cutting, 114
Beam ceilings, 23, 24–25, 160–67
    installing, 164–67
    layout, 162
    nonstructural, 162–63
Bisecting an angle, 48
Block plane, 49
Border panels, 96
Borders, 60
    linear, 62–63
    repeating pattern, 64–65
    stencil, 41, 66–69
    wallpaper, 12, 42
        estimating, 72–73
        installing, 75–77
Bradbury & Bradbury
        (www.bradbury.com), 12
Brad guns, 54, 55
Brushes, 40

C

Cathedral ceilings, 132
Caulk gun, 38
Caulking, 143

Ceiling domes, 82–83
Ceiling fixtures
    domes without, 82–83
    medallions around, 15
    recessed, 20, 21
        preparing, for installation,
            153–57
Ceiling frames, assembling, 88
Ceiling medallions, 78–81
    installing, 81–82
Ceilings
    acoustic tiles for, 18, 43
    beam, 23, 24–25, 160–67
    cathedral, 132
    coffered, 23, 26, 168–79
    color of, 60

color-washing for, 12
dropped, 28
faux finishes for, 12
glazing for, 12
height of, 28
installing molding for, 86–87
marbleizing for, 12
plank, 19, 132–39
preparing, for wallpaper, 73
rag rolling for, 12
repairing minor defects, 60
solid-color, 60
sponging for, 12
stippling for, 12
suspended, 18, 92, 94–98
textured finishes for, 12

tin, 23, 140–49
  tray, 26
  types of treatment for, 10–29
Ceiling tiles, 18, 99–101
  acoustic, 18, 28–29, 43
  installing, 100–101
Chalk line, 33
Chandelier, medallions around, 15
Chisels, 49
Circular saw, 37
Clamps, 49
www.classicceilings.com, 23
Coffered ceilings, 23, 26, 168–79
  designs, 170–71
  installing, 172–79
Coffers, tools for, 46–57
Color, ceiling, 60
Color-washing for ceilings, 12
Combination square, 32
Compound miter saw, settings for cutting crown molding, 112–13
Compressor, 54
Coped joints, 114
  cutting, 115
Coping saw, 46
  using, 114
Cordless drill/driver, 38
Cornices, 16, 102–31
  assemblies, 104–5
  built-up molding profiles, 105
  common molding profiles, 104
  defined, 104
  designs of, 16
  for indirect cove lighting, 126–31
  installation, 108
    inside corner joints, 114
    outside corner joints, 108–9
    scarf joints, 109
  materials, 106–7
  oak, with dentils, 116–21
  pine 6-piece compound, 122–25
  tools for, 46–57
Cove lighting, 21, 22
  cornice for indirect, 126–31
Crosscutting jig, constructing, 91

D

Dead-man freeze, 44
www.decoratorssupply.com, 15
Dentils, oak cornice with, 116–21
Design, creating, 27–28
Domes, 15
  tools for, 44–45

Drill bits, 38
Drop cloths, 39
Dropped alcoves, 28
Dropped ceilings, 28
Drywall finishing, 158–59
Drywall hoist, 44
Drywall saw, 36

E

Embellishments, 27

F

Faux finishes for ceilings, 12
www.fauxwoodbeams.com, 25
Federal style houses, 27
Files, 46–47
Finder, stud, 87
Finger-jointed moldings, 106
Fluorescent light fixtures, 22
Folding stick rule, 32
Framing square, 32, 89
Frieze, using spiral anchors to install, 118
Furring strips, installing, for tin ceiling, 144

G

General tools, 32–39
Georgian style, 27, 104
Glazing for ceilings, 12
www.goceilingmedallion.com, 15
Graph paper, 34

H

Hammer, 34–35
Handsaw, 37
www.historichouseparts.com, 15

J

Joints
  coped, 114, 115
  scarf, 109
Joists, 29

K

Knotty pine boards, 19

L

Ladders, 39
Leather gloves, 42
Levels, 33, 43
Light fixtures
  domes without, 82–83
  medallions around, 15
Lighting, 21
  accent, 21
  ambient, 21
  cove, 21, 22
    cornice for indirect, 126–31
  fluorescent, 22
  preparing recessed, for installation, 153–57
  task, 21
  track, 21
  xenon, 128
Lincrusta, 12
Linear border, installing, 62–63
Log homes, beamed ceilings for, 25

M

Marbleizing for ceilings, 12
Masking tape, 41
Measuring tape, 32
Medallions, 15
  tools for, 44–45
Medium-density fiberboard (MDF)
  molding profiles in, 86
  for moldings, 106–7
  for plank ceilings, 19
Mill file, 42
Miter saw, 50, 86
  cutting sprung moldings with compound, 111
  cutting sprung moldings with simple, 110
Modifications, structural versus surface, 27–28
Molding profiles
  built-up, 105
  common, 104
Moldings, 16, 17, 84–91, 111
  assembling ceiling frames, 88
  constructing crosscutting jig, 91
  cutting, for outside corners, 108
  finger-jointed, 106
  installing ceiling, 86–87

installing polyurethane, 88–90
MDF, 106–7
polyurethane, 107
sanding, 56
sprung, 110, 111
types of, 86

N

Nail guns, 54, 55
Nail sets, 34–35

P

Painted stencil designs, 13
Paint for ceiling, 12
Painting tools, 40–41
Paint techniques, 58–69
    borders, 60
    linear borders, 62–63
    minor ceiling defects, 60
    repeating pattern borders, 64–65
    solid-color ceiling, 60
    stencil borders, 66–69
Pans, 45
Paste brush, 42
Pine 6-piece compound cornice,
        122–25
Plane, block, 49
Plank ceilings, 19, 132–39
    installing, 136–38
    types of, 134–35
Plate joiner, 52–53
Pole sander, 45
Polyurethane moldings, 107
    installing, 88–90
Pop-rivet gun, 43
Post and beam construction, 132
Pry bars, 36
Putty knives, 36

R

Rag rolling for ceilings, 12
Rasps, 46–47
Recessed ceiling fixtures, 20, 21
    preparing, for installation, 153–57
Rollers, 40
    covers for, 40
Router, 52
    table for, 53

S

Saber saw, 51
Safety considerations, 57
Sanders, 56–57
Sanding screen, 45
Saw
    circular, 37
    coping, 46
    drywall, 36
    hand, 37
    miter, 50, 86
    saber, 51
    table, 50
Scaffolding, 39
Scarf joints, 109
Sconces, 21
Sheet metal, working with, 143–44
Simple miter saw, cutting sprung
        moldings with, 110
Sliding adjustable bevel, 47
Sliding compound miter saw, cutting
        sprung moldings, 111
Smoothing blade, 42
Smoothing brush, 42
Soffits, 20, 150–59

design of, 152
drywall finishing, 158–59
installing linear borders, 62–63
preparing recessed fixtures for installation, 153–57
tools for, 44–45
Spackling putty, 60
Specialty tools, 40–45
Spiral anchors, using, to install frieze, 118
Sponging for ceilings, 12
Sprung moldings, cutting
with simple miter saw, 110
with sliding compound miter saw, 111
Squares, 32
Staple gun, 43
Stencil borders, 41
installing, 66–69
Stippling for ceilings, 12
Straightedge, 81
Structural beams, 24
Stud finder, 34, 81, 87
Surface decoration, 12
Suspended ceilings, 18, 92, 94–98
fastening runners to wall track, 98
installing, 96–97
tools for, 42–43
wall tracks for, 43

T

Table saw, 50
Taping knives and pan, 45
Task lighting, 21

Textured finishes for ceilings, 12
Tin ceilings, 23, 140–49
installing, 145–49
furring strips for, 144
tools for, 42–43
types of panels, 142
working with sheet metal, 143–44
Tin snips, 42
Tools, 30–57
for acoustic tiles, 42–43
for coffers, 46–57
for cornices, 46–57
for domes, 44–45
general, 32–39
for medallions, 44–45
painting, 40–41
for soffits, 44–45
specialty, 40–45
for suspended ceilings, 42–43
for tin ceilings, 42–43
wallpapering, 42
for wood beams, 46–57
Track lighting, 21
Tray ceilings, 26
Trusses, 29

U

Utility knife, 35

V

Victorian style, 23, 27, 70, 104, 142
Visual impact, 24–25

W

Wallpaper, 70–77
adhesive for, 72
Art Deco pattern of, 70
Art Nouveau pattern of, 70
Arts and Crafts pattern of, 70
borders
estimating, 72–73
installing, 75–77
borders for, 12, 42
for ceilings, 12
design options, 72–73
types of, 72
Wallpapering tools, 42
Wall tracks for suspended ceiling, 43
Web sites
www.abbingdon.com, 23
www.americanceilings.com, 23
www.classicceilings.com, 23
www.decoratorssupply.com, 15
www.fauxwoodbeams.com, 25
www.goceilingmedallion.com, 15
www.historichouseparts.com, 15
www.armstrong.com, 19
www.bradbury.com, 12
Weight-bearing beams, 27
Wood beams, tools for, 46–57

X

Xenon light strips, installing, 128

photo credits

All photos by Neal Barrett unless otherwise noted.

page 1: courtesy of Fypon page 2: courtesy of Armstrong page 3: courtesy of Fypon pages 6–7: courtesy of Armstrong pages 8–9: *left* courtesy of Lindal Cedar Homes *right* courtesy of Fypon page 10: *top* and *bottom* courtesy of Fypon page 11: Mark Samu page 12: *top* courtesy of Fypon *bottom* Jessie Walker page 13: courtesy of Fypon page 14: Jessie Walker page 15: courtesy of Focal Point Architectural Products page 16: courtesy of White River Hardwoods/Woodworks page 17: *top* courtesy of Fypon *bottom* courtesy of Balmer Studios page 18: courtesy of Celotex page 19: *left* courtesy of Fypon *right* courtesy of Georgia Pacific page 20: courtesy of Fypon page 21: courtesy of Crystal Cabinet Works page 24: *left* courtesy of Mannington *right* courtesy of LG page 25: *top* courtesy of Crystal Cabinet Works *bottom* courtesy of Fypon page 26: *both* courtesy of Fypon page 27: courtesy of Lindal Cedar Homes page 28: *top* courtesy of Fypon *bottom* courtesy of Celotex page 37: *top* Gary David Gold page 50: Gary David Gold page 53: *bottom* Gary David Gold page 54: Gary David Gold pages 56–57: *left* and *right* Gary David Gold page 61: courtesy of York Wallcoverings page 73: courtesy of Seabrook Wallcoverings page 74: courtesy of York Wallcoverings page 83: courtesy of Fypon page 92: *top* John Parsekian pages 94–95: courtesy of Armstrong pages 96–97: John Parsekian page 99: courtesy of Armstrong page 107: top courtesy of Fypon page 135: *top* courtesy of Mannington *bottom* courtesy of Kraftmaid page 139: *bottom right* courtesy of Merillat page 140: *top* John Parsekian pages 142–143: courtesy of Armstrong page 144: John Parsekian page 152: *both* courtesy of Armstrong pages 158–159: John Parsekian pages 162–163: *left* courtesy of Fypon *right* courtesy of Merillat page 170: courtesy of Merillat page 171: courtesy of Crystal Cabinet Works page 180: courtesy of Kraftmaid page 181: courtesy of Armstrong page 182: courtesy of Armstrong page 184: courtesy of Merillat page 185: Mark Samu page 187: Jessie Walker page 188: courtesy of Armstrong

Have a home improvement, decorating, or gardening project? Look for these and other fine Creative Homeowner books wherever books are sold.

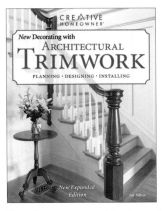

Transform a room with trimwork. Over 550 color photos and illustrations. 240 pp.; 8^1/$_2$" × 10^7/$_8$"
BOOK #: 277500

Great ideas for using molding and trimwork. Over 1,000 photos and illustrations 256 pp.; 8^1/$_2$" × 10^7/$_8$"
BOOK #: 279402

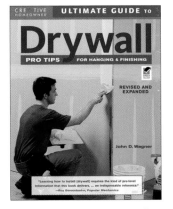

A complete guide covering all aspects of drywall. Over 450 color photos 160 pp.; 8^1/$_2$" × 10^7/$_8$"
BOOK #: 278320

Includes step-by-step projects and over 630 photos. 272 pp.; 8^1/$_2$" × 10^7/$_8$"
BOOK#: 278632

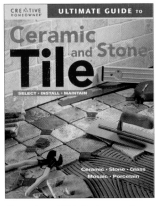

Complete DIY tile instruction. Over 550 color photos and illustrations. 224 pp.; 8^1/$_2$" × 10^7/$_8$"
BOOK #: 27753

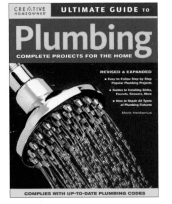

The complete manual for plumbing. Over 750 color photos and illustrations. 288 pp.; 8^1/$_2$" × 10^7/$_8$"
BOOK#: 278200

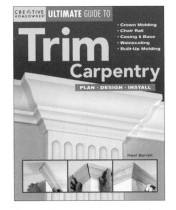

Best-selling trimwork manual. Over 500 color photos and illustrations. 208 pp.; 8^1/$_2$" × 10^7/$_8$"
BOOK#: 277516

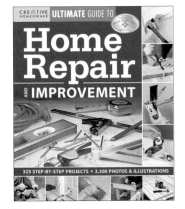

The ultimate home-improvement reference manual. Over 300 step-by-step projects. 608 pp.; 9" × 10^7/$_8$"
BOOK#: 267870

An impressive guide to garden design and plant selection. 950 color photos and illustrations. 384 pp.; 9" × 10"
BOOK #: 274610

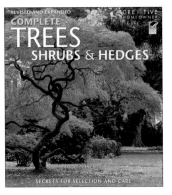

Lavishly illustrated, with descriptions of over 1,000 plants; more than 700 photos. 240 pp.; 9" × 10"
BOOK #: 274222

Foolproof guide to selecting colors. Over 300 color photos. 304 pp.; 7" × 9^1/$_4$"
BOOK #: 279648

Make a difference through everyday choices. Over 200 color photographs. 256 pp.; 6^1/$_4$" × 9^1/$_4$"
BOOK #: 277083

For more information and to order direct, visit our Web site at www.creativehomeowner.com